10/21/24

10/20/24 Blank Sonon 25.50

CHARLES NORTH
NEWS, POETRY and POPLARS
POEMS / SELECTED PROSE

BSE

ISBN: 979-8-9860369-2-2

BSE Books are distributed by
  Small Press Distribution
  1341 Seventh Street
  Berkeley, CA 94710
  orders@spdbooks.org | www.spdbooks.org
  1-800-869-7553

BSE Books can also be purchased at
www.blacksquareeditions.org and www.hyperallergic.com

Contributions to BSE can be made via our website.
To donate by check send to:
  c/o Margaret Galey
  PO Box 1401
  Lexington, KY 40588
  (Please make checks payable to Off the Park Press, Inc.)

To contact the Press please write:
  Black Square Editions
  183 Fishkill Avenue, Unit 1
  Beacon, NY 12508

An imprint of Off the Park Press, Inc.
Member of CLMP.

Publisher: John Yau
Operations/Production: Margaret Galey
Design: Shanna Compton

Cover art: Meindert Hobbema, *The Avenue at Middelharnis*, 1689. Oil on canvas.
103.5 × 141 cm. The National Gallery, London. This work is in the public
domain.

Contents

New Poems

III

I

Interview with Martin Stannard

MS: I want to begin in what is perhaps an unexpected place, by re-ferring to an essay you wrote in 2014—"The Threat of Poetry"—in which you are discussing, not for the first time, the ways in which critics approach poetry, and in there you mention William Carlos Williams's "To a Poor Old Woman", the relevant part of which I'll include here—

> munching a plum on
> the street a paper bag
> of them in her hand
>
> They taste good to her
> They taste good
> to her. They taste
> good to her

and you say, among other things, that part of the reason the poem "is as original and delightful as it is ... is what Williams *gets away with* [your italics] in that second stanza." And a few days ago, I was reading in the New Poems of your 1999 *New and Selected Poems* the following:

French Notebook Threatened by Writing

1. The day is broader than the night though more foreshortened.

2. The moon sleeps in its fully realized breadbasket.

3. For they exit via a kind of enchanted lobby pulling down housing starts—still housing starts have made something of a recovery if not nearly enough.

4. Even now your breath is volcanic to this music it sounds like Mozart—or very early Beethoven.

5. Fields with a thin winter glaze on them above and beyond.

6. The day is broader than the night.

7. The moon sleeps in its fully realized breadbasket.

And when I read that I thought immediately of the Williams comment, because here you are in #7 repeating #2, and while I could appreciate there might be any number of ways to account for that repetition through conventional critical approaches, I get the sense that you enjoy that repetition *partly* because, on the face of it, it's doing something you are not really supposed to do, especially when this is a kind of list, and lists don't usually repeat things, but *you get away with it*. I'm reading into this one aspect at least of your approach to the writing of poems. Now you can tell me I'm way off the mark . . .

CN: I like your beginning in *medias res*, which suggests we're embarking on an epic (we can make it a short one), and I think you're on the mark. I've always liked seeing what I can get away with, in lists and in many other kinds of poems (actually, I don't think of "French Notebook" as primarily a list, though of course in one sense it is). One list poem that comes to mind is that early one dedicated to Paul (Violi), "The Brooklynese Capital," which is composed of *Beowulf*-style "kennings" or periphrases almost all of which are so roundabout and unnecessary that they're close to preposterous (and interesting, I hope, at least partly because of that): "The critic of peace," "Mortality's reiterator," "The smegma convention," and of course the title. One of my inspirations from the start has been to do things that haven't been done, or at least that I haven't done, in the hope that surprising myself will surprise/interest a reader. So to me it's not just "getting away with" (in the sense, say, of sticking it to the Establishment), it's trying to produce interesting work. By the way, not everyone would agree that Williams is getting away with anything in that second stanza. I've read commentary that sees the repetition as mere emphasis, i.e., a contributor to *meaning*, never mind how surprisingly casual and even conceivably "accidental" the repetition and lineation are (I've always wondered whether WCW tried out three different line formations and decided to keep all three, which wouldn't surprise me); accident being something the critics I'm taking to task are at pains to rule out as a resource for "true poets," which is of course simply ignorant.

MS: So this approach, which I assume you will agree is to do with what I think can be called "sensibility"—I'm wondering: I know you began writing poetry in Kenneth Koch's workshop at The New School (I'm not sure what year), and then attended Tony Towle's workshop at The Poetry Project at St. Mark's (again, I'm not sure of the year)—I'm wondering how much of this sensibility you already had or *knew* you had, and how much was something you picked up from those people, and from other poets you met, or if you *discovered* it was how you felt, and I guess I'm wondering just how you found your way, as it were. I'm aware you trained as a classical musician, which does seem likely (to someone who knows nothing about training as a classical musician) to involve going about things very differently. And if you want to say what drew you to Kenneth's workshop in the first place . . .

CN: The *getting away with* is certainly one of the things that inspire me to write; I'm not sure it qualifies as my approach, or "sensibility," which to me is a large term covering whatever is distinctive about a writer's style, aims, means, etc. I'll say more about it below, but I think music (another large idea!) is at least as central, perhaps even more so.

This is how I found my way to Kenneth and poetry, essentially a series of false starts—with a happy ending. As an undergraduate I majored in English and philosophy, but philosophy was what excited me and I had no special interest in poetry. I did write, and publish in the lit mag, some prose fiction. After college, I enrolled in a master's program in English and Comp Lit at Columbia (which, if I stayed to get the PhD, would lead to teaching), but I wasn't happy and left before doing the MA thesis. The next false start was Harvard Law School, which I dropped out of after six weeks (I finally did do the master's thesis.) I then got into a PhD program in philosophy (aesthetics) but never enrolled. While working as a copyeditor for a publishing company, I wrote a handful of poems and showed them to my advisor at Columbia. He liked them and suggested I take a poetry writing class at The New School (a small college in downtown NYC with a socialist history) given by his Columbia colleague Kenneth Koch. Koch had been moonlighting at The New School for several years and, as it happened, the semester I enrolled (fall 1966)—after putting it off for a year out of sheer timidity—was the last one he taught there.

It sounds dramatic, but stumbling into Koch's class changed my life. He was the best teacher I had ever encountered and the best teacher of poetry writing this country has ever seen—I'm by no means the only one to think so. He was extremely well read, passionate about good poetry whether it was written by Whitman or Rimbaud or Lorca, or his pals John Ashbery and Frank O'Hara, or the obscure David Schubert. He made no bones about his dislike of most of the poetry that was being published in America (his early poem "Fresh Air" is a funny, trenchant satire on same) and read to us—and had us read—poets he thought would inspire us. And yes, in terms of what passed for poetry in America in the 1950s and into the 1960s, a lot of his assignments and "poetry ideas" involved getting away with things, breaking rules (as did much of the

American poetry that came to light in the early 1960s with the publication of Donald Allen's *The New American Poetry*). Write a poem that doesn't make sense (the mind makes sense of all it reads). The "flavor of ideas" in a poem can be more important than the ideas themselves (which everyone knows anyway). One's dumbest feelings are great material for poetry. Once you rid yourself of whatever you thought poetry was, it can become fun to write again. Etc.

It was all new to me and extremely exciting and I wrote a ton—at least during the course—very much influenced by his approach. Whether I had an inchoate rule-breaking gene in my DNA is hard to say, although the academic experience of poetry which left me cold certainly was fertile ground for the new to take hold. Although I kept writing poems, I didn't do very well after the class, and began to think I wasn't cut out for poetry after all. Three years later in spring 1970, I stumbled—clearly my way of moving in those days—into a poetry workshop Tony (Towle) was giving at The Poetry Project. I didn't know Tony, but he was already one of my favorite poets, and I knew he had taken Kenneth's workshop himself and had been close to O'Hara. Meeting Tony turned out to be the second magical event to do with poetry. He encouraged me tremendously, introduced me to people on the scene, chose me to give a reading at the Project, sent a poem I wrote in the class to my poetic hero Jimmy Schuyler, and perhaps above all convinced me not only that I could write but that a life in poetry/art was an important one. And Paul was in the class, too; we were soon a threesome and met regularly, showed one another poems, collaborated, etc. Interestingly, I think I first heard the term "sensibility" from Tony. At the time, he seemed to me to know everything and everyone! His taste and the rule-breaking in his own poems were important inspirations.

Of course I discovered things on my own, too, e.g., my early poems in the form of baseball lineups, which of course got away with a lot. I wasn't supposed to be giving Wordsworth's "Resolution and Independence" (which was not my favorite of his poems) a place in a baseball batting order or a position on the playing field.

MS: And music?

CN: I played clarinet in orchestras and concert bands and chamber music groups as a teenager (some alto sax too) thinking that might be my life; I stopped at 17. I once said in an interview that I write prose in some musical way having to do with rhythms, cadences, lengths, stops and starts, etc. I think—I find it hard to talk about—that something similar goes on when I write poems. I recently did a radio interview in which the interviewer misremembered my saying something in print about my poetry having gotten sloppy. What I had written, about 15 years before, was that I thought my poems had gotten "messier" (with the quotation marks)—not sloppy and not messy but "messier," by which I meant that I was letting more things into poems; they weren't as orderly or as tidy as when I was younger, which I thought was a good thing. An example I gave was the long poem "Cadenza"; the poems were now freer, more cadenza-like. But I care a great deal about line breaks and line lengths (*States of the Art*[1] has an essay devoted to Schuyler's lineation), as well as about how a poem begins and ends, flows, cadences, "transposes"—all, to me, partly musical ideas and very hard to talk about—as well as how a poem looks on the page. In fact, I spend a lot of time deciding whether something is good enough to be in print, and I don't publish very much. One other thing to do with music and sensibility comes to mind. I had the idea early on of trying to make lyrical poems out of material that is the furthest thing from lyrical; to write, as I thought of them, "technical lyrics." I have a fair number of poems that I still think of in those terms. One other thought about them, which I've never mentioned or written about, is a little fancier. There's a Freudian (Anna rather than Sigmund?) phenomenon known as *displacement*: repressed emotions, feelings, etc., popping up where they have no business doing so. Correct or not, I've always liked the idea that feelings may be unconsciously transferred to subject matter and language they have no overt relation to, and retain their feeling content on some level via the music of the language. Whether that's meaningful, or wishful, or a big stretch, I think it has something to do with poetic sensibility, at least in my case.

MS: I didn't mean to imply that *getting away with it* was your only approach! But I think it's connected with the idea that the possibilities of poetry are wide open which is, I assume, something we would take as a given, and which you touch upon in talking about Kenneth. I'm interested in what you say about the lyric, because among the questions I had lined up was to ask you to say something about the lyric poem as you see it, and I'm reasonably sure that what you say about "the music of language" and "feeling" has a truth kicking around in it that I know I'm absolutely not qualified to discuss much further without getting way out of my depth. Your philosophy studies beat me on that one, for sure. But I was also planning to ask you about the idea of your poems having become "messier"—because when I first encountered your work the best part of 40 years ago (40!) I had a distinct impression of often quite short, and seeming to me at that time—when I should add that I was very much a newbie, discovering poetries new to me—very almost "chiseled" constructs. For instance, one of the first poems of yours I published in *joe soap's canoe* in 1983 was "Descant":

Piano and hedges
and more piano
and sometimes the piano wins.
And sometimes the taxis are movie locations
    set apart from the double
    vision of the city elevatedly
    affixed to see. From storefront
    to riverfront, and from
    middle-income housing mismanagement
    to the unstabilized, stable
    poor. The bits of piano
    coating the hedges, turned
with only an occasional cloud to spill,
to fix the objects that would be there if
they weren't; powder blue and vertical
rather than one limit in a vast evening field.

So at that time, for me, I was struck by the shape of the poem (a shape which several of your poems adopted, I think), how it was put together, and also not only by how you get from the first line to the last, but what the reader is invited to think about between those two points—points which are actually not very far apart in terms of the time it takes to read the poem. (This "invitation to think" is something I want to come back to. I hope I remember!)

But in 2000's collection *The Nearness of the Way You Look Tonight* there is "Day After Day the Storm Mounted. Then It Dismounted," which stretches over a dozen or so pages, and the title poem of 2007's *Cadenza* runs to ten pages, and that book also contains the long "Summer of Living Dangerously," which takes the (ostensible) form of diary entries, mainly in prose (so you are obviously a real poet! and I know that to describe them as mere "diary entries" almost verges on the insulting, because they are far from that), and now the title poem of the new book, *Everything*,[2] is around 25 pages . . . I'm not even sure what my question is to be honest. I guess it's just about how you see your work over the years, how it's developed. I am tempted to ask, in the manner of someone who simply doesn't get it, "What's it all about?" but I daren't . . . so I will cut this last sentence out (maybe).

CN: I like the word "chiseled," and I stand corrected. When I wrote that my poems were getting "messier" (in a little statement for the Foundation for Contemporary Arts, which gave me a grant in 2008), I explained messier as "freer and more inclusive." But yes, less *formed*, too, in any sense of the word. The early baseball lineups were obviously my concoctions, but I also tried villanelles, triolets, rhyming couplets, chain rhyme (!)—in all of which I was, at least as far as I was concerned, trying to be lyrical at the same time I was being formal and breaking rules, e.g., a "philosophical" villanelle ("April"), a triolet hidden in a longer poem ("Typing and Typing in the Wandering Countryside," whose title may ring a bell), a poem composed of unconnected, fragmentary, rhymed couplets ("Fourteen Poems"); along with other quasi-formal arrangements like a poem made up of short, titled sections whose titles are part of the overall poem ("The Dawn"), and those odd, vaguely son-net-like 16-liners, individually ("Tinker to Evers to Randomness," "Detail") and grouped ("Building Sixteens," where each section ends—and then continues on). My friend the poet Larry Fagin said that the stanzas in "Building Sixteens" reminded him of bricks as well as of capital I's, which to me nicely connected odd lyricism to odd form. As to your wonderful question about getting from the first line to the last and "what the reader is invited to think about between those two points," I'm not sure I can answer—or, actually, that I would want to. To me, that's the poem's territory not mine. My guess is that this will be of no help whatsoever, but after talking about "making 'lyrical' poems out of material and language that have no business being lyrical" in that 2008 statement, I added: "I'm also particularly interested in the borders between conven-tional meaning (or meaningfulness) and what is sometimes called language play." (I didn't, by the way, and don't, mean to associate myself with the so-called language poets.)

The diary form of "Summer of Living Dangerously" was at least as much a way of organizing a long poem as it was actual diary, a way of keeping a long poem going. I think—I don't really remem-ber—that the dates are real, at least as regards the days I wrote (or began to write) the "entry" underneath. But I think it's pretty clear that it's not really a diary in the sense that any of the diaries or even poets' diaries we know are. I do, by the way, love Schuyler's diaries, which are the real thing, as well as John Clare's and a number of others; probably Schuyler's were in some sense an inspiration for the poem. Actually, and I haven't thought about it for a while, it was indeed a summer of living dangerously. Kenneth was sick with the leukemia he would soon die of. I had just had an aortic valve replacement—serious surgery requiring a heart-lung machine and, as someone said afterwards when I had reported how depressed I had been, a literal "out of body" experience—and spent that summer recovering; I was shaky not only physically but emotionally. You didn't ask, but I think there's a fair amount of "dark" material in the poem, and the ending, which on the surface is about one of the great modern philosophical formulations (by the philosopher Saul Kripke), is, to me, more importantly about the illness and death which were in the air that summer. What was the question?

MS: Hold on, I forgot—let me check back . . . Oh, it was to do with how you see your work having developed, but I think you may have answered it. At least, you've almost certainly gone some of the way, which is fair enough. I'm going to go back to the "thinking" thing, because I reviewed *Cadenza* back in 2007, and talking about the title poem I said, "It's a poem that thinks, and makes you (the reader) think too. I'm not sure one can ask for more. Actually, one can ask for much more. You can ask not just for a thinking poem but a poem which also is at the same time a delight and a pleasure to read, a poem that makes you feel you are doing something decent and intelligent with your brain and your time. And that the something you are doing is happening because you are a person who actually enjoys doing something decent and intelligent with their brain for no reason other than the doing's sake. Perhaps poetry makes nothing happen except to make the world a richer place and the people who are touched by it a little richer also."—which, at the time, I thought was a decent thing to say, and I still think so today. And in a recent review of the new book at *hyperallergic.com*, John Yau wrote that ". . . the reader can drift along, lost in the precise pleasures of North's writing, the acuity of his thinking, and the range of resources he effortlessly draws upon ("Everyone knows that Janus Weathercock and Cornelius Van Vinckboons are too good not to be true, but very few know of their connection to the poet John Clare"). If that sentence doesn't make you want to scurry to *Wikipedia*, you'd better get the oximeter out and check your pulse . . . it is not the destination of the poem that matters, the final revelation or feel-good message, but all the different ways the poet gets us there."[3] And I think the two connect up. And I'm not even sure there's a question here except, perhaps, it's got us to *Everything,* and here's a simple one (or two) about the title poem: were you planning a 25-pager when you started out? Was there a plan, or did you, for example, go fishing (to coin a phrase) with an idea to see what might happen? And I'm going to pluck out a small section of the poem here for readers to get (I hope) just a sense of how the poem moves along (not an easy thing to do, by the way)—

> You say tomato
> and I say everything is consumed by its appearances.
> I've been instructed to push
> a handful of minor characters back into the wings but
>   they won't go,
> no matter how hard I try.
> The pencil line between being and not being, hardly
> static however it looks
>
> —more accurately, between staying put
> and erupting into feelings that can't be held in check no
>   matter what,

like the corruption built into medical advertising
aimed directly at the TV-viewing public—

reminds me of the boundary line
between so-called feeling and so-called understanding.
To have a purchase on. Know thoroughly
by close contact with, or long experience of,
as opposed to hearsay or even legitimate authority. . . .

I hope you can remember the question(s).

CN: I can! You went easy on me this time. Yes, I did set out to do
a (really) long poem. With the "Study" that precedes it and the
"Coda" following (the first of which I had planned on and the
second of which just happened), it's actually more than 30 pages
both in manuscript and in the book. And I had the idea from the
start of dividing it into sections, which would, I hoped, give it some
sort of organization (not a *form* this time) even if the organization
was as much nominal as real, as well as enable me to "restart" the
poem from time to time and help keep things fresh. Thirty pages
is a lot, and the challenge, obviously, was to keep it not only going
but engaging—stimulating, moving, offbeat, on-beat, funny, sur-
prising, thoughtful, silly, everything; or, if I can say so without
sounding grand, everything we humans find our lives, inner and
outer, to be. I spent most of a summer doing the original writing,
then came back to it on and off.

Speaking of "Everything," I had the title and the epigraph before
I started, too. To me, the poem title as well as the title of the book
are on the outrageous side, and I got a kick out of that. And I loved

the epigraph from *Krazy Kat*—"Everything is just nothing repeated"—which I felt gave me the license—well, more than that; I would say a good deal of the inspiration—to see if I could let the poem go wherever it wanted, touching on the ordinary and even the trivial as much as—really a good deal more than—on what's usually considered important or "poetic." This is the Kitchen Sink principle. One of my poet friends told me I did it, wrote a poem about everything! Which I was happy to hear, even though I took what he said with a big grain of salt. But the hope was, and is, that close to nothing can play an effective part in a long poem if the part is written effectively. With respect to your wonderfully generous (actually, quite eloquent) review of *Cadenza*, the hope is that a "thinking poem" can include what isn't often material for much thought and somehow be stimulating because of that.

MS: I have to admit that part of the reason I asked about the long poem is that recently I had a long poem I wrote early last year published as a book, and in manuscript it was 30 pages, and it wound up as a 40-page book (Did we tie? or did I beat you?)—I wrote a page a day for a month then spent another couple of months "fixing" it. And I had like an "idea" and though I probably didn't go full "kitchen sink" it wandered and ranged, I think, while I kept a certain fixed point in mind all the time. I'm fascinated by process, or what (if anything) is in the mind when starting out on a poem—at least, I'm interested in process when it's a poet I admire; the opposite applies, of course, for poets and poems I have little or no time for. But, and this is a fairly boring question, but I'll throw it in anyway, if only to see how you respond: the idea of letting the poem go "wherever it wanted" is very dangerous, isn't it? (I know where I'm going with this train of thought, by the way, but one question at a time . . .)

CN: Clearly you beat me in page count (and I'm eager to see your poem). Have to try harder next time . . .

As to letting a poem go on—which to me doesn't mean "full kitchen sink" exactly (though I like the phrase) but does involve the unconscious and its messiness or lack of organization—I think more in terms of risk than danger. I know the two are close, but "risk/reward" is a familiar enough idea, whereas danger has a more ominous ring, at least to me. I remember Kenneth talking about poetry's capacity to be more interesting, exciting, etc., than other sorts of writing—or than one's ordinary speech or thinking or reasonable self—because its music, lineation, etc., encourage access to the unconscious. The reason I don't think this sort of letting go is dangerous is that, whatever emerges in the process, you have the freedom to do whatever you want with it afterwards: not only shorten, lengthen, rearrange, substitute for, but chuck it into the wastebasket.

My experience may have little relevance to yours or anyone else's, but in doing "Everything" I wrote tons, not every day because that's never worked, but enough so that I had, I'd guess, twice as many pages as the published poem. And I did what I usually do, which is put it all aside till later, give it (and me) a chance to cool off. Ultimately—I don't remember exactly—I'll bet I went back to it on and off for a year, not in any regular or planned fashion (more messiness; less method). I wonder if this idea, which just occurred to me, helps. I think I treat the original draft at least partly as raw material or resource, with the expectation that I'll go on to do whatever I decide makes the poem better: use a dozen lines from this page, use one line from that page, throw away these whole pages—which clearly happened frequently. One of the audience questions during that live stream reading[4] you saw a few weeks ago was how one revises without destroying the poem's "original flow." My answer, which I wish I had articulated better, is that one doesn't owe anything to the first (or second or third) draft; the only obligation is to oneself, to come out with a poem one likes enough to show to others in the hope they'll like it, too. In my own experience, even the flow can emerge during the revising/fooling around with stage. So—back to your question!—the only *danger*, as I see it, lies in not letting what emerged cool off sufficiently so that you can see how to make it better. The corollary as far as risks are concerned is that if you don't take them (or at least think you're taking them), the chances of getting anywhere near poetry's "magic" are much diminished. Here are two notes I kept from Koch's 1966 workshop. "There will be time for pruning once you get the orchard growing." "If you only write re what you understand, your poetry won't be more interesting than your conversation or your prose." I'm not offering these as a defense of what I've said above. But I still find the advice inspiring.

MS: Me too. It's brilliant. And it leads me (at least, I'll say it does) to where my thought train was heading, which is something to do with the probably vague area of self-confidence and trusting one's own judgment. And of course I know actually that for the most part this all comes with the years and experience and suchlike, as well as acceptance and respect from one's peers, and I suspect it doesn't hurt to have some arrogance too, along with a healthy dose of self-doubt, but one of the things that particularly interested me about your reading in that live stream was that you chose to read "French Licks," which is eight pages of translated "fragments" from a variety of French writers. And though I know they are *your* translations, it struck me as interesting that in the framework of a relatively short reading you devoted a substantial part of it to other writers, which in one sense at least is a defying of expectations (which is perhaps my subject here)—in this case, it's the audience's expectations. I think what I'm flailing around and trying to get at is that, as an artist, one has ultimately to do what one wants and feels is right, as opposed to what might be expected, even when it comes down to what to read at a public event, and I'm closing in on the combined attributes of "self-confidence" and "selfishness" here, albeit clumsily. There's no question here. I think it's more of a "Discuss." (And if this makes no sense at all, throw it back at me.)

CN: Of course it makes sense! But I'm not sure if what I say will be quite what you expected. For one thing, self-confidence has never been my strong suit. When I began, even with Tony's or Paul's blessing (we showed each other a lot of what we were doing before showing anyone else), I had trouble submitting work anywhere. I gave readings, but by no means calmly. My first book, *Elizabethan & Nova Scotian Music*, came about because Larry Fagin, who edited *Adventures in Poetry*, asked to see a manuscript I was planning to self-publish. As to arrogance—which I believe, or at least have trouble not believing, isn't my problem—of course one sees a lot of it. But whether it genuinely helps or hurts isn't clear, at least to me. It can certainly get in the way of useful self-doubt.

All that said, I do think I have more self-confidence these days, partly, as you suggest, because of acceptance, respect, etc. I wasn't going to read "French Licks" originally; it's on the long side (as you know, I did wind up cutting it a little short) and we had decided on 15 to 20 minutes apiece. I wasn't thinking about audience expectations; I just decided the poem would be easier to grasp for the listening audience (almost 200 people, by the way, invited primarily by the bookstore) for whom a lot of my work would be new. In fact, I came close to choosing "Desk," the longish one to Kenneth, but felt it, like many others, was somehow better on the page.

About "French Licks"—and feel free to delete this if you don't find it interesting enough—I think of it not just as translated snippets—or jazz licks or riffs—but as a work on its own. That could be wishful. But I spent time choosing, arranging, thinking about "rhythms" and "cadences" and beginnings and endings; what I always do. And speaking of self-confidence, I began it as hesitantly as I've ever begun anything, going through books and anthologies and scribbling (literally; you should see the notebook) translations of what struck me and in addition seemed graspable enough for me to give it a try in English. I had published two or three translations in my life, and here I was planning to dedicate a series of translations to my friend and fellow poet Ron Padgett, one of the best translators we have. I'd say, self-doubt plus chutzpah. Even when it was finished, it took me a while to show him. So when people, including Ron, told me how much they liked it, I was as much surprised and relieved as pleased.

MS: I think it's great, and it's certainly much more than simply fragments or snippets (great word). I also love the way long works like that—and I'm including the poem "Everything" in this—they can be read as a whole, and should be, but they can also be dipped into and still give the reader something interesting and, I can't avoid this word, pleasurable. I will never underestimate the value of reading pleasure.

At which point, I'm wondering if we shouldn't be thinking about winding this up. But you'll notice I haven't mentioned painting—which is mainly because I know somewhere in another interview you said that people usually mention music and art in relation to your work, and the fact that you're married to an artist, Paula . . . so I more or less determined to avoid it. But it takes only a brief look at some of your poems to see there's something of a painterly thing going on in there a lot of the time. And these kinds of interviews/conversations usually end with the interviewee being asked either (a) what are they working on these days or (b) who are the young up and coming poets they know who they would recommend we check out—and usually they get asked both. But I'm not going to ask you either of them.

Do you want to say anything about the role of painting in your work, or anything about anything else, or shall we depart the virtual room gracefully?

CN: In retrospect, it's easy to see how a connection between my poems and painting came about. It wasn't only Paula's work, which I adored, or the tons of gallery shows we went to when I began writing; painting was in the air. As I mentioned in that one-sided "interview" you published in *joe soap's canoe* years ago[5], many NY (School) poets had connections with the art world—as reviewers and critics, collaborators, curators, printmakers, drinking buddies, etc.; the poetry/painting nexus seemed the most natural thing in the world. The art critic and editor Peter Schjeldahl, whom I was friendly with and who was still writing poetry, invited me to write for *Art in America*, which I did on and off for several years. And the poet who initially meant the most to me (and whom I took cues from) was Jimmy Schuyler, a painterly poet if there ever was one. Once I got to know him (through Tony) we coedited the two *Broadway* magazine/anthologies combining poems by NY poets with drawings by NY artists including Alex Katz, Nell Blaine, Jane Freilicher (who did cover and drawings for my first book), Trevor Winkfield, Rudy Burckhardt, Joe Brainard, Rackstraw Downes, Fairfield Porter, etc.

I guess what I mean is that I came by the painting connection "honestly." But I don't think I qualify as a painterly poet, even though a good many poems have been inspired by art in one way or another, and landscapes (outdoors as much as in art) have been important to me since I was a kid. I can see that "Crepuscule with Paula" (in *Everything*), as well as others, are on the painterly side. But my feeling is that in spite of the outdoors that finds its way into a lot of poems, my real interest isn't—as a good part of Schuyler's is—in picture-making.

How about my departing the virtual room by gracefully evading the two questions you didn't ask while managing to get them down anyway? I'm thinking about working on a small book of poems with drawings by my friend (and multiple collaborator) Trevor Winkfield. And one of my all-time favorite books of poems was published by the *then* (1968) young, up and coming poet Jeremy Prynne, *Kitchen Poems*. Both, as you'll notice, English!

MS: Yes, English—at least, technically... I think by painterly I mean it's the way in which often in your poems we "see" New York, for example:

> A small apartment building with a crowded
> Starbucks at street level,
> two Korean grocers sporting green awnings,
> shadows flying in pieces out of a tinted bank window like
>   ticker tape

which is an eye for color and detail... And, by the way, I have the second of those *Broadway* anthologies—I have no idea where I got it from, perhaps from Bob Hershon at Hanging Loose—and it's one of those volumes I can pick up when I need reminding, as I do on occasion, that there's life and energy and a reason for doing this poem stuff. And although we both have one foot out of the virtual door, I'm just going to ask you about Prynne, because while *Kitchen Poems* is a Prynne I can read and enjoy, there's a lot of him I find simply—what's the word I'm looking for?—not "unreadable," but certainly "unenjoyable." And actually, having glimpsed a couple of poems from his most recent pamphlets, perhaps "unreadable" *is* the right word. I think there is just an imaginary line where on one side the work can be experimental or innovative or whatever word one chooses to use but it's still open and possessing a human element that allows the reader in, and on the other side there's just words, which seem too often to be saying not much more than "let's see what you can make of this," albeit under the guise of "interrogating or dismantling the language" or whatever, to which my reaction would often be to go and do something else. And I guess I'm not just talking about Prynne here, but a lot of "innovative" poetry. Any thoughts? Then we can both get out of here...

CN: Yes, in that sense of painterly I would agree, even though I really think it's for you to say and not me. You should hunt down the first *Broadway* too (wonderful cover by Paula North, in addition to the poems and drawings; if I had a copy to send you, I would).

I knew you weren't going to let me get away with that passing reference to Prynne! I think your points are well taken and well put, and I know others who feel exactly as you do. I was bowled over by *Kitchen Poems*—talk about "getting away with." What I found most engaging and original if not magical about those poems, as I did about a good bit of the early work collected in the Agneau 2 *Poems* (1982), was their *sub rosa* (sometimes not so sub) lyricism. In addition to the dogged cerebrality, "interrogating and dismantling the language" as you put it, the poems contain the traditional stuff of poetry: things, feelings, dailiness, weather, landscape, political climate, history, *music*. What you call "the human element." I'm pretty far from the English poetry scene and haven't seen much of what's been written about Prynne, but it does seem to me that the dismantling has gradually swamped the rest. I sometimes kid around, though I don't think I've done so in print, about "The Revenge of Poetry"—you know the 60s horror flick about poets who never swerve from their original discoveries. Or was the title "The Cliff of Diminishing Returns"? Like everyone else I have poetic heroes; but the poems by them that really inspired me would stop coming, sometimes before the poet turned 40. Diminishing returns seems especially applicable to "language oriented" poetry. As exciting as it can be—and I've tried to do some myself—in my experience a little goes a long way. Prynne succeeded for longer than anyone might have expected, as did the little known American poet Joseph Ceravolo. But I'm counting on the fingers of one hand.

MS: Oh, Joe Ceravolo is wonderful. But let's leave readers to find him for themselves. Charles, thank you.

["An Inteview with Charles North," Litter Magazine, UK, 2021]

Notes & References

1. Charles North, *States of the Art: Selected Essays, Interviews, and Other Prose 1975–2014* (Pressed Wafer, 2017): https://www.spdbooks. org/Products/9781940396354/states-of -the-art-selected-essays-interviews-and-other-prose -19752014.aspx

2. *Everything and Other Poems* can be found at The Song Cave: https://the-song-cave.com/collections/new-items/products/ everything-and-other-poems-by-charles-north

3. John Yau, "The Writer as Citizen of the World," Hyperallergic (May 3, 2020): https://hyperallergic.com/559885/ everything-and-other-poems-by-charles-north-song-cave/

4. The reading hosted by the Paula Cooper Gallery, and also featuring poet Vincent Katz, took place on May 19, 2020, and can be viewed here: https://paulacoopergallery-studio.com/posts/ poetry-reading-with-charles-north-and-vincent-katz

5. Charles North, "The N.Y. Poetry Scene / Short Form" can be found in joe soap's canoe #8 (May,1983), and is archived here: http://www. martinstannard.com/jsc/jsc8compressed.pdf

6. Charles North, "Charles North on 'Piece of a Rhapsody'": https://poetrysociety.org/features/in-their-own-words/ charles-north-on-piece-of-a-rhapsody

II

Poems from *En Face*

Poem

I thought it was going to be personal.
—I'm trying. You can never
really tell, subject lines after all have feelings too
like headphones, endpapers, etc.

On the other hand the trains make both local and express
    stops
since all parts are played at all times, including
the ones that "silently partner" in their own destruction
if I can say that.

The salad bar sits with a view of the headstrong Chrysler
    Building
while the line of gray benches has a self-destruct feature.

John Clare Lineup

10 a.m. Super Blush
4 p.m. The Italian Bugle
with the flared moorings (and stagecraft).
When Fillinghams Tantarara tangles with leaf green
everything smells of Lilac Flowered Bergamot.
Browns Lord Hood is on p. 347.
Lookers Oxonian steps up to the plate
with the operatic sling. Hugh's
Pillar of Beauty takes on the stream
coruscating like a medicine cabinet in December
as Morning Star comes about, nudging
Miss Greens Pink into the poem.

Clere Parsons

So we're not yet reformulated into Old Master
paintings with inks and the occasional reference
to forces co-existing with human possibility
however careening like wind into late sun. O openness!

Just say the word before the stars drop
their coals onto the rust-colored doormat
given the plush that throbs and the nervous months grouped
and assigned their responsibilities, distance and thrall.

Limits of Outdoors

How the roar of a motorcycle
isn't equal to love

any more than puffs of chimney smoke dotting the boroughs
reach out to the earth's imagined corners.

—There are five boroughs.
You think I don't know that?
Or that I don't take every other word out of my mouth
with a grain of salt, if not a tablespoon?

Even the relatively healthy window plants know what they're
    about
without a hint of egg tempera or baroque halos
that look like gold dinner plates.
By Andrea del Verrocchio. Foothills with bands of trees
and a far-off mountain like a pale blue breast.

En Face

Arrows blown against the mull day
war is a meal.
Who gradually plucks
and who with noise raised
can edge a tantrum?

For volition and essential
with the ordinary beef
swarms like heads. A fist
accountant chimes as late as
proverbs lose.

Ersatz clover wore to Corniche frond.
Recall a vicinity cruise
while vent closes the tag.
A basement love, a tithe
loss of timber to ruin mince.

And evenness bikes up
through livestock meeting regularly.
An example plays Stern
above or cutting past each fret
and foundry rule to flacon.

(For Harry Mathews)

Penguin Books
Direct flight to Key West

November 13
The saloon of the poem

O Lower Extenders
O reckless fire hydrants and coffee shops!

#3 Pencil
Hand Holding Asparagus

Then in French
Middle darks, dry and powdery, 6 p.m., almost

A La the 1940s Movie Lobbies
With standing ashtrays

John Clare 2

Before the light and chalk stop, one or two fingertips
glued to keys so what has to be done takes its cue
from the dream state with its endless car chase,
the fakebook practicing scales (smell of rain),
the wild hurry of the autumn clouds.

Fishing

into the evening especially if you
don't count the twig-like intimacy or the front matter
that would sneak out of the *Collected Poems* if it could—
if no one was looking—whatever the cost
to the facts of the matter and their less than resourceful
cross-hatching amounting not exactly to tree shade but thick
enough to imperil the passage from now to then
****

front matter plus the bluffs and prominences, taller
than the ornate tower on the Municipal Building

Poems from *Translation*

Poem for Trevor Winkfield

Two mops are cavorting in the next world.
"What do you do?"
"Nothing! I don't do anything!"
Orange light, then darkness. Then orange light.

(1982)

Jig

A pair of Swiffers are doing a jig in the Afterlife.
"How do you spend the time?"
"I don't! It passes."
A burst like a marigold. Then nothing. Same again.

A Note on Labor Day*
for Paula

Sometimes I think I'm
close to discovering
why half my life has occurred
in a fog, which makes
the other half radiant
by comparison.
The wind,
September's ship,
blows some pigeons
out of a blue and white voiceless fog
off the cornice. Another
flock, atmospherically vague,
is flowing east: a rather pale gleam
with fragments of a greenish metal
embedded in it, among
them a starfish complete
with notes on its history.
Musical ones.
And I seem to be
lost again, if that doesn't
sound too dramatic,
and this time seems worse,
or around the slightly silvered bend
slightly blurred in late sun
that has some whirling filters over it
mostly for the jackets and the books.

Poem

On rare occasions it seems to me
that I'm onto myself,
why so much (of everything)
has been dull or blank—against which
what's left shines.
A breeze shouldering
the end of summer
brings a few pigeons
back to life from
their perch near the roof.
A few others (harder to see)
head towards Amsterdam
Avenue: a thin stream of light
like a patina with
sea green particulates
(notes from past as well as
present) reinforcing it.
And if I can say it
without seeming histrionic,
the feeling of not being
any place I *know*
is back, this time in
spades: like spending months
inside the walls of a migraine.
The Volkswagens and Toyotas
hug street level with

The cars
stay close to the ground
to be near the trucks.
The buses and taxis move heaven
and earth to be near anyone.

*Lines 1–31

(1978)

its commercial vehicles.
Yellow cabs and the occasional Broadway bus
home in on people.

Nocturne

The gods are fighting to stay awake. Just now one hurled something over the drawn-in end of the river below. Everything is subsumed, the sleep of landscape, the flowers in the window box existing when no one is looking, the street with its bone china and animadversions towards roots of daylight. Time stops gamely. A large bloodshot eye encircled by small gray cumulus clouds behind a white shade, a smudge near Mercury, towers at the far end of the spectrum: an inverted pyramid of cheese, tomatoes, and extra cheese. Moments hurtle through over and below open and closed windows scattering crystals, roars of houseplants. The far piling marbled with green and white light, transfixing the northeast, is Discord.

(1987)

After Chopin

The superheroes can hardly keep their eyes open. One flings a hunk of gray metal across the Hudson River, curled in a fetal position. Nothing is omitted: the dreaming park with its unoccupied benches and walks, the geraniums unobserved, thin side streets pointing hopefully towards dawn. Space to Time: No you may not! An orb spattered with red inside a gray gaseous frame, atmospheric distortion nudging the core, the office buildings watching all of downtown: a slice of pizza overloaded with toppings, wobbling on its point. Exceedingly small units of time burst past the kitchen curtains breaking plates and glasses—and the crystalline silence. A long way off, in the region targeted by nor'easters, Chaos aims its ray gun.

French Notebook Threatened by Writing

1. The day is broader than the night though more foreshortened.

2. The moon sleeps in its fully realized breadbasket.

3. For they exit via a kind of enchanted lobby pulling down housing starts—still housing starts have made something of a recovery if not nearly enough.

4. Even now your breath is volcanic to this music it sounds like Mozart—or very early Beethoven.

5. Fields with a thin winter glaze on them above and beyond.

6. The day is broader than the night.

7. The moon sleeps in its fully realized breadbasket.

(1992)

Cahier Menacé par l'Ecriture

1. The hours when the sky is blue are compressed yet substantial.

2. A crescent of white light curls up like a breakfast roll in its straw container.

3. Here one minute gone the next. Not much in the way of new building but some fortunately.

4. After so much—you and the night and the Classical tonality but with a sense of Romantic surging just around the corner.

5. Hard flat land frosted where you can see as well as further on.

6. The hours when the sky is blue are the substantial ones.

7. A crescent of white light curls up like a breakfast roll in its straw container.

Urban Landscape
for Ron Padgett

What if
instead of growing
older
we rose,
a few inches
a year, until
approximately
double mature height,
passing every
manner of person
against a background
of windows,
walls, cars, posts
and tree trunks
between the sidewalk
and the second story—
sun
inching down,
clouds strung out overhead.

(1988)

Suspension

Suppose
mortal life
had spatial and
not temporal bounds,
each person
inching upward
to a maximum of, say,
6 ft. off the ground
such that
the city air
framed by the natural
and also man-made
objects one notices
while walking up
a city block
is filled with
far more people
than a Magritte painting—
the sun appearing
to descend
in tiny increments
towards the region of fixed clouds.

New Poems

Synopsis

Try squeezing it into a Concord grape. There's your wine-
   dark sea.
—I did that already!

Even when I try not to think of you
it's as though your being for want of a better word
is pushed out to the tips of my fingers.
Sandwiched, to put it another way, between hope and what is
   hoped for.

I would like to write a song in detective style,
how procedure plays in along with legwork and the shattered
   daylight industry
as a result of the war felt if not quite experienced,
the difficult air and feelings holding on.

Maybe—maybe you're the one driving the Land Rover Defender
   over the narrow bridge. It looks like you.
Air and a sweep. In sum: the parietal lobe
but also those doing the talking (and fishtailing),
from early avatars to present-day wing motifs.

Ode

Antique fire engines, chicory on a kitchen table

O July

clinging not so much to people as to their plates and
    glasses
from a fragile enough sense that things
pile up, regardless of time
or the space that inevitably closes around it.

Saussure phoned ahead about the *gloss* not the glass.
The side street with the ATM window has a thin patch of
    city grass
trod flat by shade from a ginkgo tree with a branch
like a bent finger—

Please pay attention.

It doesn't have to be a 1940s movie lobby
filled with standing metal ashtrays
or the chorus line decked out
in flame-colored taffeta.

The sun backs into a Starbucks window
(seersucker collar, medium braids, the Avenue at
    Middelharnis

pushing its way past painterly lights,
appealingly awkward uprights

Thus: upper and lower extenders slash
away at what can be written
before the city on file, quietly flaming ginkgos
but also vegan restaurants with a surprising number of
    regulars
at the outdoor metal tables,
sets down its non-negotiable terms for the ode
to us, formal and musically complicated.

From the Italian

Mentalese O divided
love of things—your
soil frame for example in the room
for the slow passage.

Since outwardness plays
right field and the
emotions of small city streets, green and talkative
until they coast.

Liner Notes

5/18.   (5:10 a.m.). Not such a strange time to be up when you think about it. Not littered (not all there, but what is).

5/29.   What do window treatments really know? However Edward Hopperish or even Vermeerish.

6/2.   Dizzy Trout, Harry (The Cat) Brecheen, Hippo Vaughan, Rabbit Maranville, Moose Skowron, Goose Goslin, Ducky Medwick, Catfish Hunter.

Fenton Mole!

6/3.   A messy day not sloppy. Almost no room anywhere— clouds, hedges, paint, captions, etc.

6/6.   The heartfelt peonies and their unavoidable connection to the inner life. The paint thins out the closer you get. Paper, some posterboard—unlike thought and its thin bed (romaine, leaf lettuce, spinach). Restless as a side street or the thinly quilted afternoon wondering (obsessing?) about coffee and whether to have an early dinner rather than wait till after the movie. The mourning dove underneath the A/C practicing the tune, how hard can it be.

6/9.   A Renaissance Progress. Make it a Convoy.

6/10.   All the reds including blood oranges to give a hint of the future which isn't that far away. You have the right to remain unlike *anything* nameable or not. Freight elevator with faux brass paneling, the afternoon of the coleus, superhero chess piece (knight) with folded cape and surprisingly heavy boots.

6/21.   Stadium lights by 6:00.

6/23.   How do you know it hasn't ended already? (How would you know if it had?) Snoop the cat has a leg up on dreamtime. The orange hawk—more of same—came back along with its hand-painted background, barely visible through soot streaking the window pane. Quivers in her sleep. Waltz? Polonaise? Mazurka??

Polonaise.

Trio for Christian Wolff

Brooklyn for Hours

Trying not to display carabinieri
folds afloat. Are sirens
reinforced with basic
wading but the dream throws its rocks!
Such ground. At the announced
ten years of what's left for the spot
folds of form vs. prescience. Bolder
distilled Vienna
pre-cassation, Le Nôtre.

Brooklyn on a Column

Sheep flag
fresh from shreds
and waxing despite people—the
Venn mall.

Wads as well as holes needing to be filled
being the exoticism of keeping.
By aspect if not. I worry about
hospital architecture is what it convenes
when it is loud or curtain blue.
In ninths underneath.

Brooklyn Tone Row

Known or pine.
The squeezed glass
for viola d'amore and magisterial
vatic enough: twist potato
Mesozoic tint cabinet.

As in each. The haunt
crossing aspen seas
crab don or skin.

Each somewhat
at the clip being cold—?
To harbinger, a peony
usual stop them. Belong
blas causerie.

Eyefuls

Small ones from the 96th St. crosstown bus
to be boarded iff the aggressively cantilevered building racing
to enclose the sky over Broadway the way
Enclosure invaded England as early as the 12th century
is the world view.
Doucement por favor.

Periodic Table Etude

for Anselm Berrigan

Harmonium, Ding an sich, Capo,
Caesura, Herculaneum, Albritton (for John Koethe),
Lovage, Claritin, Deus ex Machina,
Proscenium, Tympanum, Hap, Emporium,
Rose Water, Rigid Designator, Haroosh, Polymorphism,
Likeness (for Paul North), Ergonomics, Omnium Gatherum,
Dickinsonium, Duration, Feldman,
Petitio Principii, Delerium, Nature Morte,
Lament (for Ignacio Sánchez Mejías), Alexandrine, Impasto,
Aspen, Sub Rosa, Pandemonium,
Cadmium Red Light, Nostrum, Heartsease,
Pericardium, Resurrectine, Eau de Vie.

For Bob Hershon (Ode to Ed Head)

rf	Don Gullett
ss	Pinky Higgins
cf	Leo the Lip (Durocher)
1b	Ed Head
3b	J. J. Putz
lf	Rollie Fingers
rf	Wally Backman
c	Nate Oliver
p	(Walt) No-Neck Williams

****

dh	Hack Wilson
	Lance Berkman
	Horace Stoneham
	Waite Hoyt
	Louis Lepke

Liner Notes 2

8/19.   Wheeling and dealing (Sibelius).

8/20.   The gargoyles in their dark green, flannel (velvet?) PJs with the black piping. Nothing about who gets to speak and, more importantly, who doesn't.

8/23.   Flaneur my foot. The sliver of moon in front of a full-length bedroom mirror (dancing to W. C. Williams).

8/24.   To the future tense (improv) rather than the past (Grosse Fugue/late quartets). The no-shows not only don't have to pay their dues on time, but they get to watch on live stream for nothing!

8/26.   Blue, period. As in the lined clarinet case with both clarinets, cork grease, swab, Dutch rush, extra reeds, etc. The plush sets up the blue range. I don't mean oceanic—or windswept—but the buzz and the microtones didn't come out of nowhere. Then a brilliant phrase. Another on top of it.

8/30.   Didn't they used to call linguistic tropes flowers? What likeness has going for it even where there's no obvious agreement about purposes or means. I like the notion of lateness as a trope in and of itself. The gargoyles slept in, clambered down too late to do anything let alone glare at the endless traffic.

8/31.   A heart in the middle lane, which is bumper to bumper as far as I can see. Adolescent smudges and blades turning the corner into the cantilevering of middle age and all the rest. The noir: pretty much as advertised apart from the lush foliage and then it ends.

Haibun

O city air   O foliage   nothing is *there* never mind if it smudges

Take the book with no cover hard or soft (in all but a couple of versions), the angel with the beak zeroing in on the Museum of Natural History framed by leafy side streets (unlike the dive bars with their ceilings out of *film noir* and eyelashes giving feeling a run for its money)

O historical breeze, lives shy as fingernails, the impulsive crows

Transcendental Etude

That one
including the sedan of slopes
waking up in the middle of a tone row.
Try sadness I did.
No you didn't you "framed" the idea.
The nap of reason along with 10-foot cornstalks
like vertical sunbeams.

It's brushed then it settles.
It isn't historicism it has time
on its side never mind the seasons
which don't take a step without consultation
surface detail or anyone's!
Does history have practice sessions?
June's come-hither rose
between sorrow's technicals
—tux, cotton canvas, smudge of hard times—
as much. The cornstalks on their cells.

The Furies knew where to eat and drink.
Regards to the peonies and their inner life
(which didn't accept them the last time).

Wind, Intermittent Rain

How about blowing *everything* away
including the dialogue meant for someone else (I'm almost certain)
and the asterisks that take up unnecessary room
since they aren't stars in spite of all the attention from below

not to speak of the impulse as palpable as a hawk on an air
   conditioner
to look farther than the eye can see, beginning with show balconies
a foot wide (if that) to the Art Deco spandrels nobody looks at
to the half-hidden transoms and mullions that hold up this
   painterly life.

March Note

How difficult is it even beauty takes a look
from its rooftop. To lie down for a week or even two
while the mourning dove practices its major and minor
    scales
on the kitchen window ledge as pale as a hospital.

First (French) Licks

Elegance? Give it a chokehold.
And while you're at it
Sit rhyme down and pour it a double latte.
Otherwise who knows what it will be up to.

—Paul Verlaine

These wraiths, or are they women, how to hold onto them?

—Stéphane Mallarmé

Drink, sleep, die—you need to save yourself from yourself
In any way that's humanly possible.

—Oscar Vladislas de Lubic Milocz

Where are the old sorrows
The ones from last year that I barely remember?
If someone came in right now to ask what is it,
Is anything the matter,
I'd say I'm all right just leave me alone.

—Francis Jammes

The scrawny afterlife, black with its gold trim

—Paul Valéry

What's going on on the pier? In French. *Merci.*
Bonjour. Adieu. It must be getting late.
Here comes the robin who sings to me.
Blacksmith's hammers in the distance.
The water laps. A stertorous steamer.
Enter one fly. In and out breath of the sea.

—Victor Hugo

I need to go higher I can still see
The stockbrokers in their granny glasses,
The critics and the spinsters,
The realists with their red faces.
Higher still. Farther. Blue air.
Wings! I need wings!

—Théodore de Banville

The honeysuckle breath of their beds

—Alphonse de Lamartine

O I loved you . . . as a lizard shedding its skin
Loves the sun that roasts it while it lies sleepily . . .
Love between us beating its wings . . . Hey!
You! Get out of my sunlight!

—Tristan Corbière

84

I'm smoking, spreadeagled, nothing but night sky
On top of the coach,
Jostled at every turn, my soul dancing
Like some Ariel—
My beautiful soul in its dance, no honey or gall,
O roads and little hills, O smoke, O valleys—
My beautiful soul, all we once had!

—Jules Laforgue

For David Schubert

Grief doesn't have all the answers
yes or no.
Nothingness that trio sonata
across the leafy street with the four o'clocks
simmer down.

Lyrics of the Trouvères

Demain! Not much of a glass.
So-called legerdemain padded by you know what
in the direction of Auteuil, a #3 pencil
implacable as a first aid kit.

Thus nothing is spotted with war or pine trees.
Futurism's grove in which we skulk
in recognition of which differential diagnoses
take a nap in December worrisomeness.

Reliquary dreams below.
If you leave without the control,
shoulder to shoulder like pats of butter,
the truculence is on the stargazer side.

What godsend fiddles with sadness? Careful about
cheekbones, eyelashes over the Atlantic.

George Smiley

in the cornfield along with the husks
and splintered baseball bats (I almost said *smitten,*
as though late p.m. in October were
Endymion's moon and not just a windy compound)
plus the risk-tolerant deer, cagey woodchucks,
crows, and even the occasional wild turkeys
on their way home from school

—all of which darken perceptibly
but don't stop. Reading stops.
Like the fictive voice which the French use
for their weather (*Il fait*) so the subject
takes on a cloudy presence but no reference,
sans agency sans intrigue sans whereabouts.

Fifteen Poems
for Barbara Friedman

History
Slept in

Paolo
Uccello!

Muffed
"In the pro" tranche

End Around
Tense as an asterisk
risky as a ballpoint pen
pensive as Chopin
(*pangs*) rare as Cage (missing)
Sing, Muse, of the disconsolate past tense

Scare Quotes
It isn't "brushed"

Erato
O Muse of Typographical Errors
(grace notes in her medium-length, wavy brown hair)

Do Sycamores Shiver in October
Picked not quite clean
like the carcasses along the twisting Taconic

Upshot
Hebrides #2 which must be 1954? Thinner than endive.

Petrarch
Silk root

Homage to Morton Feldman
The Selmer A and Bb clarinets in my life

End Around 2
Ode to winter
turning (leave *some* air!)
mares' tails over the pebbly road

The Noisome (Silver) Bay
Of quality

Two Gargoyles Take a PM *Walk*
Whether quoins are an embrace
or sentries in the thickening air

Mere Alcohol
A one-horse town

The Stale World
Call back

Fragment of a Memorial

Chairs with bamboo arms and legs, fingers
(thin but made of flesh and bone) and the lake of the past gleaming
  like a Mozart Rondo.
The musical life? When the sun drives within the speed limit
and place being what it is makes room for time's grace notes,
beside the white chickens.

III

School Ties[1]

1

Was there—and is there—a New York School of poets as there was a New York School of painters? At this point, to me, the answer is a clear no but yes. The original group, Kenneth Koch, John Ashbery, Frank O'Hara, James Schuyler, and Barbara Guest (Edwin Denby, Kenward Elmslie, and Harry Mathews also belong if not so centrally), were much more friends and kindred spirits than a "school." Their poems didn't—and don't—seem very much alike. They weren't interested in poetics per se and they issued no manifestos. And yet they were a group whose writing differed markedly from the rest of American poetry in the 1950s, and whose spirit and aesthetics have carried over into a second generation and beyond. If it's still difficult to say what a particular poem by Ashbery has in common with a poem by Koch or Schuyler, there are nonetheless useful generalizations to be made about shared likes and dislikes, ways of approaching their art, and connections to New York City, which, despite its relatively rare appearance in their poems, was central to their development—as it has been for the significantly larger second generation.

One of the things that united the first generation in the 1950s was their reaction *against* the conventional poetry in the literary magazines and in prominent anthologies like Robert Pack, Donald Hall, and Louis Simpson's *New Poets of England and America* (1957). In "Fresh Air," a rousing early poem/diatribe, Koch decried poems "Written by the men with their eyes on the myth / And the Missus and the Midterms." O'Hara's joking but serious prose piece "Personism" (1959) admonished poets not to fall back on rules or habits but rather to "just go on your nerve." Years before, Ezra Pound had directed poets to "make it new." For the New York poets this meant looking to Europe rather than America for models: adventurous modernists like Apollinaire, Reverdy, and Mayakovsky along with their great predecessors Rimbaud and Mallarmé. A handful of American poets had made it new, among them Whitman, Pound, Gertrude Stein, William Carlos Williams, Hart Crane, Wallace Stevens, as well as virtual unknowns like David Schubert and John Wheelwright, but American models were few and far between.

It is well known that schools often acquire their names casually, for reasons (including negative ones) that have little if anything to do with the scholarly (and non-scholarly) uses to which the names are put. The "New York School of Poets" title was first used in 1961 by the art dealer/publisher John Bernard Myers as a way of borrowing caché from the already prominent "New York School of Painters": Kline, Rothko, Motherwell, de Kooning, Pollock, Guston, etc. But the poet-painter connection has a far more significant and lasting aspect. What most attracted the poets in the beginning was the New York art scene: not only the exciting painting, which represented a sense of creative possibility far exceeding what was evident in the visible poetry around, but the painters themselves. The poets, all strong, competitive personalities, were drawn to painters' hangouts like the Cedar Bar and the Club, where the equally competitive painters talked shop, argued, gossiped, drank prodigiously—and composed just about the only audience for their poetry the poets had. Donald Allen's landmark anthology *The New American Poetry* (1960), which placed the New York School poets alongside other groups who were in the process of transforming American poetry—Black Mountain, Beats, San Francisco Renaissance—included a brief piece by Schuyler on the importance of the art scene:

> New York poets, except I suppose for the color-blind, are affected most by the floods of paint in whose crashing surf we all scramble.... In New York the art world is a painters' world; writers and musicians are in the boat, but they don't steer.
>
> ("Poet and Painter Overture")

As it turned out, the poets went on to have professional affiliations with the art world. Ashbery, O'Hara, Schuyler and Guest all reviewed exhibitions and wrote criticism; Ashbery was an editor of *Art News* and O'Hara became a curator at the Museum of Modern Art. Even more important, not only the lives but the poetry of all five remained intertwined with art and artists, from collaborative projects to major poems like Ashbery's "Self-Portrait in a Convex Mirror" and O'Hara's "Why I Am Not a Painter" to ways of writing inspired by the paintings they admired.

Collaborating with artist friends—New York painters like Jane Freilicher, Larry Rivers, Alex Katz, and Joe Brainard—became something of a modus operandi, as it had been for the European modernists portrayed by Roger Shattuck in *The Banquet Years*. But it wasn't only the "crashing surf" of paint that was stimulating. The poets loved and were influenced by the movies too. (As O'Hara half-joked in "Personism," "After all, only Whitman and Crane and Williams, of the American poets, are better than the movies.") Koch, Ashbery, O'Hara, and Schuyler wrote experimental plays (Koch a great many) whose stagings included sets and costumes by artist friends. Koch read his poems aloud accompanied by Rivers' jazz saxophone. Mathews and Elmslie wrote experimental fiction as well as poems, and Elmslie had one foot in the world of opera and musical theater as a librettist. Denby was a dance critic (to many the leading one of his time) and his close friend Rudy Burckhardt was a photographer and filmmaker who collaborated frequently with poets. All in all, there was an important sense of poetry taking its place among other arts, an enlarged sensibility (which had already been enlarged not only by awareness of European poetry but by the presence in New York of émigré artists such as Marcel Duchamp) that stood in sharp contrast to the narrow scope of much American poetry. It is significant that the two major literary magazines the poets had a hand in, *Locus Solus* (five issues edited by Ashbery, Koch, Schuyler and Mathews—one of which was devoted to collaborative writing) and *Art and Literature* (twelve issues edited by Ashbery, the English painters Rodrigo Moynihan and Anne Dunn, and Sonia Orwell) were international in their casts and distribution and not restricted to poetry.

Collaboration, with painters as well as fellow poets, is a central feature of New York School poetry. Another is a refined wit (which was important social currency among the group as well), part of an overall determination not to be overly or exclusively "serious." It was one thing to take poetry seriously, which they all did, quite another to take oneself too seriously, or to believe that poetry must be somber or lofty or spelled with a capital P (what, at its worst, Koch in his comic and highly serious poem "The Art of Poetry" called "'kiss-me-I'm-poetical' junk"). O'Hara's pointed remark in "Personism" underlines the attitude: "I'm not saying that I don't have practically the most lofty ideas of anyone writing today, but what difference does that make? They're just ideas." A related strain is parody, overt in Koch, central if implicit in Ashbery, evident in O'Hara and Schuyler too; another is combining what might be called "high art" with "low," as in Ashbery's sestina featuring Popeye, Wimpy, and Olive Oyl ("Farm Implements and Rutabagas in a Landscape"). It should be added that many New York School poems have no trace of pop culture, parody, or indeed humor of any kind.

Certainly what makes each poet different from the others is at least as important as what they have in common. Koch's poetry through much of his career is what is sometimes termed "high concept": he has specific "poetry ideas"—arbitrary devices among them—which get a poem going and keep it running. Ashbery's resonant nonlinearity and extravagant explorations of his own complex psyche are different from O'Hara's restless romances embracing people, painting, and language (which are themselves different from his own "I do this I do that" celebrations of dailiness). Schuyler's elegantly clear-cut views of the world outside aren't the same thing as Guest's elegantly disjunctive (and increasingly fragmentary) renderings of inner and outer life. Denby's delicate sinew, Elmslie's antic wordplay, and Mathews' formal feats are each unique to the writer. As to the common elements, I find it most useful to think of the first generation as displaying "family resemblances" in the Wittgenstein sense: similarities and affinities of one kind or another, between certain poets but not all, rather than essential or necessary traits. The fact that the poets not only liked but drew on one another's work, as well as disliked so much of the poetry around—with a consequent sense, strongest at the outset, of isolation if not embattlement—is as important as what can and can't be articulated about New York School poetry. As to the recognition they all eventually received, that came relatively late and by no means in equal measure, Ashbery by far garnering the lion's share.

2

Jim Brodey, a member of the next generation, once proposed a History of the New York School from 1949–1969, and separated the younger poets into those who had arrived in the early '60s and those who came on the scene in the second half of the decade.[2] Others, Tony Towle for one, also distinguish between an initial second generation and those, mostly younger, who followed. In fact, one or two—notably Bill Berkson—were on the scene just before 1960 and formed a bridge between the generations; but in just about every respect the second generation New York School was a product of the 1960s. If there was a single key event, it was the establishment of The Poetry Project at St. Mark's Church in the

East Village in 1966 and Anne Waldman's taking the reins shortly after. Some in the group had already come together via magazines like Ted Berrigan's *C Magazine* and Peter Schjeldahl and Lewis MacAdams' *Mother*, as well as in downtown café readings and one-time events like the Berkeley Poetry Conference in 1965. But there had been nothing like the community that grew up around The Poetry Project, with which just about all the poets who came to be identified as second generation New York School had some association. There were readings twice a week; poets led workshops for other poets, who went on to lead their own; a succession of magazines and chapbooks produced on a shoestring became a Project staple, publishing (and read by) just about everyone in the community.

The establishment of a community was abetted—to a large extent enabled—by an exceedingly low cost of living, particularly in the East Village. A number of poets found cheap apartments within walking distance of the Project and lived, if not communally, then in the closest thing to a community, getting together not only to write and read each other's work, but for parties, meals, poker games, protests, and the like. Cheap apartments meant that some could get along working part-time or sporadically, reserving their energies for poetry. Those who lived elsewhere in the city or outside it had higher living expenses, which usually meant a steady job, but New York in the 1960s was still a place where poets without a lot of money could live decently and also find time and space to write. For those who lived some distance from the Village, the Project was just as much the poetry center. Though many friendships lasted, the second generation was never homogeneous and never stable—infighting and shifting relationships were a significant part of the experience. Still, there was a shared sense not only that poetry was vital but that one could live the life of a poet without compromising one's values, as well as a sense that isolation from the mainstream, poetic and general, was not only an energizer but a badge of honor.

For many who found their way to The Poetry Project, Koch had been the inspiring mentor, at Columbia where he was Professor of English from 1959 on, and at The New School where he taught poetry workshops from 1958–1966. In the mid-late '60s Berkson also taught poetry at The New School, and O'Hara—in addition to being a charismatic model for the artistic life in New York—gave his own workshop there in 1963. All three had members of the second generation in their classes. The poetic innovations of O'Hara and Ashbery (who didn't begin to teach until the mid 1970s) were prime influences for the younger poets. But there were many other influences too, not least *The New American Poetry*, which, if it wasn't quite the Bible of the New, provided stimulating models close to home—not only New York School, but Allen Ginsberg, Gregory Corso, and Jack Kerouac; Charles Olson, Robert Duncan, Robert Creeley, and Denise Levertov; Philip Whalen, Jack Spicer, and Gary Snyder; John Wieners and Le Roi Jones (Amiri Baraka); and 26 other poets who were turning American poetry in new directions. Beginning with Bob Dylan, The Beatles and The Rolling Stones, there was also the new music replete with its countercultural attitudes, aesthetics of performance, and enormous appeal—not to speak of the pro-Civil Rights and anti-Vietnam War fervor that pervaded the lives of those who came of age in the '60s. Though the first generation's work and attitudes were very much a part of the second generation, the increased range of influences encouraged the younger poets to bring their own "fresh air" to poetry. The sense of a genuine community together with the publications emanating from the Project set the second generation apart from the first, who, for all their innovative writing and collaborating, lived their own lives, mostly held regular jobs, published with known presses who distributed their work via known channels, and displayed their rebelliousness within the precincts of 1950s America. The first generation had had, for the most part, traditional schooling (Koch, Ashbery, O'Hara, Mathews, Elmslie, and Denby at Harvard, Guest at Berkeley), dressed conventionally, drank alcohol, which was the drug of choice for most of the population, young as well as old. Though there were Ivy Leaguers among the second generation (Columbia, Princeton, Brown), overall the education was less classical, there was more reaction against schooling per se, and all the vital impulses that roiled the '60s were central to their lives as well: social activism, drug-taking, folk and rock music as well as jazz, rejection of conventional work, behavior, and dress, together with a pervasive sense of solidarity, especially among those under thirty.

The Project publications are a specific case in point. *Locus Solus* and *Art in Literature*, in the very recent past, had had relatively high production values and international distribution. The mimeographed, hand-stapled, and hand-collated Project magazines and chapbooks—especially Larry Fagin's *Adventures in Poetry*, Anne Waldman and Lewis Warsh's *The World*, and Maureen Owen's *Telephone*—were put together at "collating parties" and handed out, mostly within the Project confines. Whereas the first generation magazines were selective, the Project publications were democratic and inclusive on principle. They printed work by first generation New York School poets as well as by young poets in Project workshops. In addition, they welcomed poets whose primary affiliations were with, say, Black Mountain, or the Beats, or the Umbra group, rather than New York School. Although some on the outside complained (especially at the outset) that the editorial policies were inclusive to a fault, the various Project magazines and chapbooks represented an exceptionally high percentage of the innovative work being done at the time, by newcomers as well as by those who already had some reputation.

Unsurprisingly, given the lineage as well as the size of the group,[3] it is at least as difficult to say meaningfully what constitutes second generation New York School poetry. Once again, amid great variety there are family resemblances and shared attitudes much more than traits in common. Like their predecessors, the second generation have continued to react against what is conventional or stale or watered down in American poetry as displayed not only in magazines and anthologies (including the college anthologies that reach the widest audiences) but in the vastly increased number of poetry readings and the majority of reviews and poetry-related pieces in widely circulated publications like *The New York Times Book Review*, *The New York Review of Books*, *The New Yorker*, the *Times Literary Supplement*, and the *London Review* (these publications' real strengths notwithstanding). Certainly the second generation poets have been as non-School and as unprogrammatic in their approach to poetry as the first generation. If anything, the mingling of social and artistic ties has been more pronounced in the second generation than in the first, to the degree that it is hard to say which have been more central: shared tastes led to friendships; friendships led to ways of writing; both resulted in collaborative productions, poetry magazines, readings, workshops, and the like. Although by no means everyone in the second generation took first generation poets as models, the wit, humor, mix of high and low, ambition to "make it new," and overall irreverence have continued unabated, as has the habit of collaboration. It is difficult to think of a second generation poet who hasn't done a project with or had a book cover done by an artist friend, or published collaborative works with fellow poets. A Project fundraiser in 1991 took the form of a large exhibition at Brooke Alexander Editions in New York of "Poets/Painters Collaborations." (The two *Broadway* anthologies I edited with Schuyler in 1979 and 1989 were conceived with the idea of mixing poems with drawings by artists with whom the poets had close connections.) European modernist poetry, in particular French and Russian, has continued to influence New York poets; Ron Padgett, Bill Zavatsky, and Michael Brownstein have done substantial translating from the French, and many others in the second generation have done at least some translation.

If the New York City art scene as a whole hasn't been the *center* it was for the first generation, art has remained important for the lives, work, and poetry of many in the second. Peter Schjeldahl, Carter Ratcliff, and John Perreault (all of whom turned their energies to art-writing early on), became prominent art critics, as did John Yau, who remained an active poet; and Bill Berkson and David Shapiro have done substantial art writing as well as teaching. Tony Towle worked for years at Universal Limited Art Editions; Ted Greenwald had important gallery affiliations; Paul Violi was an editor at *Architectural Forum*; Ted Berrigan, Ron Padgett, Towle, and I, among others, have done reviews and criticism. Among the poets' artist friends, Joe Brainard, George

Schneeman, and Trevor Winkfield stand out. Brainard and Winkfield have worked with both first and second generation poets. All three have done numerous collaborative projects and book covers, and have been as much a defining part of the second generation as the poets themselves. Both Brainard and Schneeman did poet/artist comics too, and Brainard's innovative prose book *I Remember* has become a classic, widely read, taught, and used as a model for younger poets.

3

Is what is sometimes called non-linearity a distinguishing mark of New York School poetry? Ashbery, Guest, and Koch (at least early in his career) pulled syntax apart, pushed asyntactical language together, made isolated words and phrases bear the responsibility of "meaning." But Schuyler didn't; and O'Hara did only a little. Joseph Ceravolo's early work, e.g., his lengthy "Fits of Dawn," sometimes appears to have originated in some other, buried language. Brownstein's early work is non-linear in Ashbery fashion, and Towle's earliest poems collage material from non-poetic sources as well as dreams. Elmslie has always cared more about words—notably their sounds and collisions—than about conventional syntax or meaning. I mention these last four because they are the first winners of the annual, short-lived Frank O'Hara Award, set up by first generation poets to honor O'Hara and to foster experimental poetry. However, the final winner, John Koethe, writes in a linear fashion, as do a number of others in the second generation. Numerous other modes and categories link one poet with another, or one subgroup with another—catalogues, conversational tone, invented forms, collage, dailiness, found poetry, "anti-poetry," pop cultural material, Dada, jazz inflection, notation, prose poetry, fragmentation, fake translation, "language-writing," ekphrasis, parataxis, composition by field, rule-breaking for its own sake, to name a few. On the other hand, many poems written by second generation poets not only display none, or few, of the above features, but make a point of *not* displaying them. One might say of New York School poetry, rephrasing an idea that was in the air when the first generation was coming of age, that rather than its existence preceding its essence, it *supersedes* it.

4

Terence Diggory's *Encyclopedia of New York Poets and Poetry* (2009) takes the New York School through at least two more generations. To my mind, whether or not the school notion survived the normalizing 1970s in a meaningful way is less an issue than a matter of alternative ways of looking, with something to be gained from both views. The focus here is on the poets born between 1934 and 1945 (Ceravolo and Ted Berrigan to John Godfrey, with an important exception for Shapiro—born in 1947 but one of the first to arrive on the scene) who were close enough to the original group personally and artistically to, in some real sense, "belong." Koch taught many of them, O'Hara directly encouraged others (and would doubtless have encouraged more if not for his early death), Ashbery inspired many, as did Schuyler and Guest—although in Guest's case, to complicate matters further, her influence on younger poets was greatest once she moved back to California and in the process lost much of her association with the New York

School. The work of all these, along with that of Denby, Elmslie, and Mathews, was just beginning to be known when the second generation was forming, and came to be touchstones at the time, a situation that didn't obtain later on. *Locus Solus, Art and Literature,* the Project publications, the *Paris Review* (with second generation poet Tom Clark as Poetry Editor), and Kulchur Foundation (Lita Hornick's press published a number of second generation poets including some first books, threw publication parties, and additionally brought poets and artists together for an annual winter bash) all contributed to a New York School spirit and a shared aesthetics, which, by the time a younger group came along in the mid-late '70s, had been diluted and transformed despite ongoing workshops, readings, and group publications. As frequently happens, the initial enthusiasts grew older and less enthusiastic, their emphases changed (some moved away from New York) and were reflected in what they passed along to younger poets, and many of the original impulses were no longer the same or as compelling as in the 1960s, when the sense of bucking a vast establishment and of doing something genuinely exciting and genuinely new was palpable. Everything felt different.

To some, none of the above means that the New York School closed shop in the mid-1970s. To others, it is more useful to think of the school idea as less meaningful after that, and instead to see the ongoing attitudes, strains, and influences—communicated by both generations—as having become part of the fabric of contemporary American poetry, as likely to make an appearance in an academic setting like a University of Iowa MFA workshop as in a reading by a young poet at the Project. If the last sounds ironic, it is because it is. Even Ashbery, now the most celebrated poet in the Anglophone poetry world, had no expectations as late as the late 1960s that his poetry would be read, much less win the major poetry prizes, or that the New York School of Poets (which title he has been known to disavow) would win a place in the history of American poetry in the late 20th century and onward.

(2009)

Notes

1. Unpublished; originally written for *New York School Painters and Poets: Neon in Daylight*; Rizzoli, 2014.

2. While not setting out to do so, *An Anthology of New York Poets* (1970; ed. Ron Padgett and David Shapiro) went some way towards charting the so-called New York School. In addition to all in the first generation except for Barbara Guest, the book included 20 younger poets—though it omitted a number who came to be known as members of the second generation as well as featuring several who "dropped out" early.

3. Whether there are 40 who count as the second generation, as Brodey suggested, or somewhere between 25 and 30, which at this point seems a more meaningful number, depends on whom you ask. The following poets are pretty much agreed on: Bill Berkson, Ted Berrigan, Jim Brodey, Michael Brownstein, Joseph Ceravolo, Tom Clark, Clark Coolidge, Larry Fagin, Dick Gallup, John Godfrey, Ted Greenwald, Frank Lima, Bernadette Mayer, Charles North, Alice Notley, Maureen Owen, Ron Padgett, John Perreault, Carter Ratcliff, Aram Saraoyan, Peter Schjeldahl, David Shapiro, Tony Towle, Paul Violi, Anne Waldman, and Lewis Warsh. Others with distinct New York School connections include Michael Benedikt, Steve Carey, Douglas Crase, John Giorno, Allan Kaplan, John Koethe, Ann Lauterbach, Lewis MacAdams, Ed Sanders, Lorenzo Thomas, Tom Veitch, Marjorie Welish, Rebecca Wright, John Yau, and Bill Zavatsky. A third generation would include Anselm Berrigan, Eddie Berrigan, Jim Carroll, Tim Dlugos, Elaine Equi, Gary Lenhart, Greg

Masters, Eileen Myles, Elio Schneeman, Michael Scholnick, Susie Timmons, and more.

Thanks to Ron Padgett for helpful feedback.

For Larry Fagin Memorial

I get some weird pangs that have to do with Larry. Whenever there's a track meet on TV (rare these days), I expect him to phone, beforehand to let me know when, or afterwards with results. He had a thing for pole vaulters, so if one of his favorites set a personal record, I got the exact height. He knew I didn't pay nearly as much attention to track and field as I used to—we both ran in high school—but that didn't matter. We were still the only people who remembered the distance runner Fred Wilt, or the longtime Director of the Millrose Games, Fred Schmertz, or the great Jamaican quarter-milers from when we were kids.

He phoned or emailed about other things, too—sports, books, movies, music, art; also specific things: could I tell him what I thought of a poem by one his students (never mind that he was the one being paid, and on top of that he was always accusing me of being too tough!), had I read the new Bix bio, did I know how good "The Rape of the Lock" is? We met at Orlin Café on 8th St. every few months, and he always came with a list of handwritten topics, as well as, much of the time, a gift: a book (he gave me the best translations of Pasternak I've ever come across), a set of vintage Bing Crosby CDs he had put together, a new jazz/pop mix he had made for Paula and me. I also had the benefit of some of his pronouncements on classical music, including some, to me, absurd ones, which I came to feel were mostly for effect. That side of Larry's wasn't my favorite, the Arbiter of Everything, but he was so interesting and knowledgeable in general, and such an enthusiast, that like those he was close to I forgave him a lot. Not, I must say, that I knew everything. Once, aware of my distant past as a clarinetist, he arrived with a mix of jazz clarinet cuts, which clearly had taken thought and time. To thank him, I did something I hadn't done for anyone else, ever: I brought my instrument to his apt. and gave him a private performance of Stravinsky's *Three Pieces for Solo Clarinet*. I didn't play it the way I did when I was 16, but he clearly got a great kick out of it, and both his enjoyment and his gratitude moved me.

I didn't know Larry well, not nearly as well as Ron or Trevor or Miles or Anne Waldman did, but he was important to my life as a poet from the time I met him in the late 1960s. He was my first publisher, who, when I mentioned a manuscript to him at one of Lita Hornick's poets and artists parties, *ordered* me not to self-publish it (as I had done with my one and only publication, *Lineups*) but to let him have a look. I greatly admired *Adventures in Poetry* but I hardly knew him at that point, so his invitation floored and of course delighted me. He wound up choosing half the poems, picked a typeface, and invited Jane Freilicher, one of my favorite painters, to do the cover. She did two drawings, too. This was *Elizabethan & Nova Scotian Music*, which I still think is a model of what a small press could do with no money and No Tech.

It wasn't only his publishing my first book; it was that Larry remained one of my encouragers. However I was feeling when I entered Orlin, I would leave convinced that poetry, music, film, art *mattered*; they were what mattered to him and it was impossible to be with him and not feel the same. If he liked something, he went out of his way to praise and in many cases to support it. One of the lasting virtues of Adventures, the magazine and the books, is that it made room for people whose work Larry liked whether or not anyone else even knew their names. Jamie MacInness and Emily Greenley were no less important than Jack Spicer or Alexander Pope. None of this precluded his being a champion know-it-all, which included, with his friends as much as anyone, putting down (or at least affecting to put down: half the time it wasn't serious) one of *your* enthusiasms, I came to feel just because you had come up with it rather than he. Pronouncements were his life's blood, or at least many liters of it, as were his official ratings for big-band singers, interior linemen in the 1940s, names of baseball players (Memo Luna and Dummy Hoy near the top), Ashbery poems.* I once committed the grievous error of praising Ella Fitzgerald. His response, after making a face, was to detail her utter lack of musicianship, all the while calling her Elephant Gerald. Not very nice but not without wit. I'm not sure everyone knows the column he wrote for the California jazz magazine *shuffle boil*, chockful of interesting info and wit, with the punning title "Polka Dots and Mean Booms." It was clear to me that side by side with his half-serious, high-level trash talk, was his always wanting to know what I was working on, always asking if I had anything for his current magazine, ordering me to write this or that, in addition to complaining that I considered (and still consider) "Self-Portrait in a Convex Mirror" a great poem.

I'll end with a small anecdote that relates to all of this, and that I hope doesn't seem self-serving. One of the striking things about Larry's last weeks was his staying Larry—at least the Larry I knew, as interested in books, art, food, life, as he always was. Trevor Winkfield and I visited him a few times at the Jewish Home on 106th St. He had heard about our recent Granary collaboration, *Elevenses*, and prodded us to let him see it. This was towards the very end, when he had a lot more to think about than books. We initially demurred, neither of us eager to lug our copy of this big, expensive book on the subway. But since Larry kept saying how much it would mean to him, we gave in. I can't remember who brought it the first time; I remember Larry's getting out of bed with difficulty—at that point he weighed about 100 lbs.—and sitting like a schoolboy at the tiny hospital table beside Trevor, who turned the pages one by one, with Larry silently taking it all in. It's a spectacular production, thanks to Trevor and to the publisher, Steve Clay, but when Larry said it was the most beautiful book he had ever seen, I had tears in my eyes. Just before we left, he ordered me to return and give him a private reading of my part. I demurred about this, too, but he insisted.

A week or so later, somewhat embarrassed as well as anxious (by this point he looked awful), I read it to him; it took about 10 minutes. The few times I looked up, sick as he was, he seemed rapt. When I had finished, he said quietly, "That's wonderful. You have to publish it on its own." "By itself?" I managed. "The art and the production are what make it, I'm along for the ride." He gave me a stare, not unfriendly, more parent to unruly child, and pronounced one of his pronouncements: "What are you talking about, *you* know you're one of the greats." Well, of course I took that with a grain of salt. But I found his seriousness together with the quality of his attention extremely moving. It didn't matter that he was dying: poetry mattered; art mattered; his pals mattered. We could have been back at Lita Hornick's party talking about my book, or in his living room with Stravinsky or Lee Konitz or Sidney Bechet.

---

*I'm taking the liberty of attaching an email (with my annotations) he sent to me one June a few years ago, which demonstrates, I think, the seriousness that underlay his endless list-making, critical ratings, kidding around, rule-breaking, really his approach to art in general. Lineup poems were, of course, my idea, and the nuances often depend on a reader's knowledge of baseball. But Larry did some things here that I never did, throwing caution (and orderliness) to the winds, somehow making his choices personal in addition to being offbeat or outrageous, beginning with "entre nous" and ending with Nathan Detroit's "So sue me," i.e., not just kidding around.

*

C,
With nothing better to do a few afternoons ago, I thought of my personal favorite lineup, *entre nous*:

    2b – Dustin Pedroia[1]
    ss – Honus Wagner
    lf – Ted Williams

rf – Babe Ruth
1b – Hank Greenberg
c – Yogi Berra
cf – Dummy Hoy[2]
3b – nobody[3]
rp – Christy Mathewson
lp – Eddie Plank
mgr – Casey Stengel
owner – Bill Veeck
bench
rp – Urban Shocker,[4] Noah Syndergaard, Mark Fidrych,
   Allie Reynolds[5]
lp – Lefty Grove, Hal Newhouser, Sandy Koufax, Randy
   Johnson
c – Mickey Cochrane
lf – Arky Vaughan, Eddie Basinski,[6] Phil Cavaretta,
   Johnny Mize, Eddie Collins
of – Pete Reiser, Carl Furillo, Ichiro Suzuki, Dominic
   DiMaggio

So sue me.
XO,
L

---

1. An odd choice right off the bat. No baseball fan I know would rate
   Dustin Pedroia over Eddie Collins or Rogers Hornsby or Rod
   Carew or Jackie Robinson, just to name a few of the greats. So
   Pedroia, an admirable second baseman if not a Hall-of-Famer, is

one of Larry's favorites for reasons we can only guess at.

2. Again, a good player if not in the class of Ty Cobb, Willie Mays, Cool Papa Bell, Joe DiMaggio. William Ellsworth Hoy played center field for a number of major league teams, beginning in 1888. Meningitis had left him deaf at the age of 3, hence his nickname—which Larry loved.

3. Wonderfully wacky; conceivably a hidden reference to Abbott and Costello's famous routine "Who's on First?" in which players have names like Who and What—except for the right fielder who is unaccountably omitted. A Selchow and Righter board game used the 8 names from the routine and called the right fielder Nobody.

4. A good if not great pitcher with one of the greatest baseball names ever.

5. Fans know the names Syndergaard, Fidrych, and Reynolds, each of whom was/is notable, but they must be included for reasons we're unaware of, especially in light of the great lp's on the bench.

6. An unremarkable player with a limited major league career. My guess is that Larry chose him because his name appears in the greatest baseball song ever (to me one of the great songs, period), the jazz pianist Dave Frishberg's ode to baseball names, "Van Lingle Mungo."

Super Moon, for P.

Last night's "super moon" (the biggest in something like eighteen years) appeared to be about ten miles away, no more, just above the east side of the East River, which was also the limit of my view from St. Luke's cardio floor where I was pre- and post-op for my aortic valve procedure in late October and early November of last year. I used to leave the shade up about a foot at night so the early light would come in, even if it didn't wake me. It wasn't an especially pretty view due East, nor did it cheer me up exactly, but I kept mentioning it when anyone phoned as though it meant a lot. For some reason it did. Curiously I didn't think at all of Columbia, only two blocks north, during the entire time I was in the hospital—twelve days—except for trying (unsuccessfully) to get Paula to walk a couple of blocks out of her way to cut through the campus on her way to and from the Broadway bus, which seemed safer to me at night than the dark side streets. She did fine on her own.

(2011)

On "Piece of a Rhapsody"

Piece of a Rhapsody

The dawn turns into a maple tree then a fakebook from the windy 1940s then back into dawn and speaks. It would be nice if writing as well as reading took a lot less time. That by the way is chapter one. With the net out, shaded in or not, and the sadder exclamations, sprocket and well-wisher, sending a pigeon as an envoy. Just in case. As for the suggestion that the natural world is no more constructed than a Plan de Paris, it was followed by a thin cloud of reddish smoke, more plum than scarlet, spattered by daylight.

[2018]

"Piece of a Rhapsody" wasn't planned as a rhapsody, or a piece of one, or a prose poem. It somehow emerged as all three, and I wound up liking it enough to publish it. I don't plan much before

I write. Mostly, I'm looking to surprise myself, in the hope that as a result the poem will have a chance of surprising the reader. This one, from a few years ago, I'm pretty sure began as a scribbled diary entry—which I can't find! I remember doing a little revising but not much.

Rereading the poem now, I see a lot of red: the maple tree (I've always been a fan of red maples), the reddish smoke, the faded red cover of a *Guide Général de Paris* from decades ago when my wife and I lived there briefly, plum, scarlet, the sun coming up. Red isn't necessarily the color of exhilaration, though it's often the color of dawn; I notice that the "sadder exclamations" with their "sprockets" (in the film sense) are at some remove, so to me at least, this was one of the exhilarating dawns.

I should say something about the very beginning, what Aristotle might call the efficient cause. There's a poem, quite obscure by now, by Keats's friend Leigh Hunt (also obscure), which I've loved since I came upon it in an English Romantic Poets course in college, "The Fish, the Man, and the Spirit." It's actually three sonnets: "To a Fish," "A Fish Answers," and "The Fish Turns into a Man, and Then into a Spirit, and Again Speaks." In the back of my mind for a long time (along with a lot of other things) was the desire to do something in the spirit of the Hunt poem. Before the dawn speaks in mine, it's been transformed into a maple tree, and then a fakebook (in the older sense of a resource for musicians, which I used to be; I suspect that's how the title came about as well). Then, as itself, it begins its poetry reading.

[Poetry Society of America "In Their Own Words." Online, 2020]

Celebrating John Ashbery

1. *90 Lines For John Ashbery's 90th Birthday*

It was always November there.

> (from "The Chateau Hardware,"
> *The Double Dream of Spring*)

What first struck me is that my copy (Dutton, 1970) has it as *Novemeber*! (The pencil line I drew through the extra *e* is still there.) I still love it as an opening line; concise and confident, it appears to introduce so much. It also sets the stage for what was to me then a new kind of language, music, and even meaning: on the "technical" or at least oblique side, paratactic, unspecific, unexpected (including the passive voice), staccato to start but capable of expanding in all sorts of ways.

[*Literary Hub*, July 2017, eds. Adam Fitzgerald and Emily Skillings]

2. *Remembering John Ashbery*

John has meant so much to me—to American poetry—that it's hard to know where to begin. The permissions he gave us all, enriching to this day, began with his first book, *Some Trees* (I still have the Xeroxed copy a friend made for me in the late 1960s when I was just beginning), continued with the undersung *Tennis Court Oath* (which remains a treasure chest of permissions despite being downgraded by critics, and even by John himself), and flowered in its fullest forms in *Rivers and Mountains*, *The Double Dream of Spring*, *Three Poems*, and *Self-Portrait in a Convex Mirror*—all, to me, among the most important books of poetry produced since the Second World War.

I was excited by a lot of poets when I began, but somehow John was my poetic hero; he still is. I remember when he was close to unknown—which was the case even in the late 1960s—apart from the few readers who noticed Donald Allen's *New American Poetry* and the poets who, like me, were in their twenties and hung around The Poetry Project. It was close to impossible to believe that his reputation would extend beyond New York City, let alone that in his lifetime he would set the record for poetry awards! In his quiet—but relentless—way, he broke too many rules. He was far too self-indulgent. What he wrote didn't sound like poetry.

I'm sure we're all lifting a glass to John, but I'm guessing he's free to drink with Raymond Roussel, John Wheelwright, Giorgio de Chirico, and even Henry Darger, whose names we might not know if it weren't for John's quietly relentless praise.

[Library of America online: September 7, 2017]

Ron Padgett's Robert Frost Medal

I'm very happy Ron Padgett is getting the Poetry Society of America's Robert Frost Medal, and very happy to be introducing him. He is one of the most engaging writers we have on and off the page, and has been attempting things in poetry no one else attempts. As a poet myself, I feel pretty much the way Billy Collins, our former Poet Laureate, did, when he wrote: "I wish he would loan me his sunglasses for a day or two so I could check out the amazing world according to Padgett."

One poet who didn't say much about Ron, as far as I've been able to determine, is Robert Frost, who wasn't shy about speaking out. I hope the following doesn't embarrass Ron. I recently heard him read his wonderful Apollinaire translations along with his own poems. After the reading, someone in the audience whose intelligence and taste I respect, stated matter-of-factly: "Apollinaire's good, but Ron's better." Blasphemy! Though I heard myself, to my surprise, mumbling in agreement. She was talking about Ron's poems and not his translations vs. the originals (and in fact, one of Padgett's strengths as a translator is his dedication to the original, insofar as that is possible). But in agonizing—er, in thinking about—this introduction, I found myself wondering what Frost, who we all know *defined* poetry as what is lost in translation, would have made of Ron's exemplary Apollinaire. For all that's *necessarily* lost from one language to another, isn't it also true that something is gained—if the translator is as good a reader and as good a poet as Padgett? If I may blaspheme just a bit myself, and paraphrase Frank O'Hara, who had more important things on his mind: Without Ron's versions of Apollinaire, would our poetry books be as full, as the earth is full, of *poetry*? I know the Frost medal isn't for Ron's translating (he has other awards for that), but I can't help tacking on a comment about Ron's Apollinaire from *Translation Review*. It's by the translator David Ball.

> When I read the poems in French, I kept thinking "Now how can you possibly put *that* into English?" Then I looked at the facing text. And thought, to paraphrase Henry Higgins in *My Fair Lady*, "By God, he's got it! He's really got it!" It's like watching a little boat in high seas: how can it possibly make that wave, and that one? But it does, easily: it just floats up and over them. Padgett makes it look easy. We translators know nothing is harder than that.

I myself have been a fan of Ron's poems since I began writing, but as much as I would like to think so, it's hard to imagine Frost really taking to them. Of course, taste is multidetermined. When he was beginning, Frost didn't have, as Padgett did, the example of

The New American Poetry, which offered permissions and models (Beats, NY School, Black Mountain, San Francisco) that simply weren't available before then. Nor, this is a guess, was Frost aware of Kenneth Koch, who as Ron's mentor changed his life (mine too, in fact) and who was, arguably, the best teacher of poetry this country has ever seen. If Frost happened to be aware of Koch as a poet, it's hard to imagine his enjoying Koch's satirical thrusts at mid-century American poetry, and in at least one instance, Frost himself.

From the outset, Padgett's poetry has been ingeniously offbeat, partly in a Dada, or anti-poetic, spirit designed to shake up things and readers, to do what you're not supposed to do. Frank O'Hara famously said, "You just go on your nerve," which seems to me what Ron does; but it just so happens that his nerve *keeps* pointing him in surprising and interesting directions. Ordinary life—the weather, a meal, friends, *dailiness*—is certainly one of his subjects, but so is poetry and how it gets written, which in Ron's case often seems to be out of thin air. Sometimes his poems are surreal, sometimes absurdist at least in part; sometimes downright goofy, other times straightforward and serious; sometimes funny and sometimes very moving; sometimes loud, sometimes quiet; sometimes tiny, sometimes quite large. Yet for all their modern and postmodern as well as purely Padgett-esque moves—for all their *nerve*—I've always detected an essential lyricism, sometimes on the surface, sometimes not showing through till the very conclusion of an otherwise zany or outrageously unconventional work. I've detected something else too, which seems to me fundamental and which isn't ordinarily included in a blurb designed to sell a poetry book: an essential good-naturedness; even—I hope he doesn't mind my saying this—a sweetness. I would say that there isn't a mean bone in his poems.

Speaking of nerve, when Ron was in high school in Tulsa in the late 1950s, he started a literary magazine and invited some big names to submit, including Jack Kerouac, who did send work—*most* of which was accepted. After high school he came east to go to Columbia, where he met Koch, won college poetry prizes, and then went off to France on a Fulbright, which marked the beginning of his translating as well as providing continuing inspiration for his own poetry, Apollinaire but also Max Jacob, Pierre Reverdy, and other European modernists. Back in NYC, again encouraged by Kenneth, he was a pioneer in teaching poetry to school children—a commonplace now, but close to unheard of then. He was also an early Director of the St. Mark's Poetry Project, and Publications Director for Teachers & Writers Collaborative, which by the way is celebrating its 50th anniversary.

How many books has Ron published, not only poetry but translation, memoir, biography, collaborations with poet friends like Ted Berrigan and artist friends like Joe Brainard and Trevor Winkfield, teaching books, editions of the works of others, even fiction? I would say at least 40, and I'm probably underestimating. I remember coming upon his first collection from a major publisher, *Great Balls of Fire*, just after I had emerged from a workshop taught by Koch, filled with new notions about poetry and how to write it. Ron's book bowled me over in a number of ways. I loved the title—I had grown up with Jerry Lee Lewis's rock song but never imagined you could get away with it as a poetry title! I also loved a little set of lively, funny, unconventional "Odes," in both English and Italian, to the poet Ungaretti, to the Futurists, to Mussolini

(!)—which opened my eyes to all you could do with forms, etc. My eyes were opened even wider by a funny poem/playlet lifted whole from a Berlitz travel language book, and by a mysteriously resonant 14-line poem all of whose lines are the same as the title, "Nothing in that drawer."

His next book, *Toujours L'Amour* (which I think remains central), completely won me over, from its title, to its back cover photo of the author as an elegant gangster, to what was inside, including a long *love* poem containing material from a seed catalog, another long one using dopey things kids write in one another's high school yearbooks, and some wonderful short poems as well, like this tiny, untitled set of three:

> I call you on
> the 'phone &
> we chat, but
> the way tele
> is missing from
> 'phone is the
> way it makes me
> feel, wishing
> the rest of
> you were here.

>   *

> In literature and song
> love is often expressed
> in the imagery of

weather. For example,
"Now that we are one
Clouds won't hide our sun.
There'll be blue skies . . .
etc." Partly cloudy
and cool today, high
around fifty, mostly
cloudy tonight and tomorrow.

　　　*

4:50 and dark
already? Everyone
wants to be
beautiful but
few are. 4:51
and darker.

Here are two more, slightly longer but something of a set as well,
to my mind quintessential Padgett:

Poema del City

I live in the city.
It's a tough life,
often unpleasant, sometimes
downright awful. But it has what
we call its compensations.

To kill a roach, for example,
is to my mind not pleasant
but it does develop one's reflexes.
Wham!
and that's that.
Sometimes, though, the battered roach
will haul itself onto broken legs and,
wildly waving its bent antennae,
stagger off into the darkness

to warn the others, who live in the shadow
of the great waterfall in their little teepees.
Behind them rise the gleaming brown and blue mass
of the Grand Tetons, topped with white snow
that blushes, come dawn, and glows, come dusk.
Silent gray wisps rise from the smouldering campfires.

*

Poema del City 2

A light chill on the knees
& I sneeze
up late, alone, in my house, winter
rain against the window and glittering there
in the constant light from stoops across the street
cars hiss down from one moment to
the next hour: in an hour

I'll be asleep. Wrapped
in new sheets and old quilts
with my wife warm beside me and my son
asleep in the next room, I'll
be so comfortable and dreamy, so happy
I'm not terribly damaged or dying yet
but sailing, secure, secret and all
those other peaceful s's fading
like warm tail lights down a long landscape
with no moon at all.
     Ah, it's sweet,
  this living, to make you cry, or rise
  & sneeze, and douse the light.

I won't read it, but I want to mention one other which I heard Ron read at the Apollinaire reading. "Do the Math" is a longish poem that makes up the text of a collaborative chapbook he did with Trevor Winkfield a few years ago. Beginning out of, or in, thin air, it gathers unlikely steam and proceeds through a sizeable range of experience inner and outer, some of it weighty, and then stops, in the most ordinary of human locations, the kitchen, with that most ordinary of human activities, lunch. It's not a lunch poem, as in Frank O'Hara, but it doesn't rope off anything as unfit material for poetry.

The following, I think, relates to the above. Among Ron's achievements, which have been piling up in recent years, is the movie by his friend Jim Jarmusch, *Paterson*, about a bus driver in New Jersey who writes poetry (and which many feel is the most accurate, and least mythologizing, depiction of a poet ever). A fan of Padgett's work as well as a former student of Koch's, Jarmusch invited Ron to be the movie's "poetry consultant" and wound up using Ron's poems, a few written for the movie as well as a few older ones, as the protagonist's. It occurred to me that at least on some level, Jarmusch may have connected his protagonist with a poet whose language and subjects are determinedly down-to-earth, with room for buses and the people who ride them, home life, walks in the park, breaks for lunch, roaches—never mind that they stagger off to their teepees—and who had the nerve not only to write an "Ode to Stupidity" but to begin it with the word "Duh"!

Ron's national prizes and other honors—somewhat like the progress of many of his poems—couldn't have been predicted when he was in his 20s and involved with The Poetry Project's outsider project of setting American poetry on its ear. There are too many honors to name, but here are a few. He is Chancellor Emeritus of the *other* poetry organization, the Academy of American Poets; one of his books was a Pulitzer Prize finalist; the French government honored his translating by making him an Officier in the order of Arts and Letters; he has a Fulbright and a Guggenheim, and awards from the American Academy of Arts and Letters and the Foundation for Contemporary Arts; he received the PSA's Shelley Memorial Award in 2009; his 800-page *Collected Poems* from 2014 won both the PSA's William Carlos Williams Award and the *L.A. Times* Prize for best poetry book of the year; he was awarded the Academy of American Poets Landon Award for Translation; he edited Scribner's three-volume *World Poets: An Encyclopedia for Students* and, for the Library of America, Kenneth Koch's *Selected Poems,* and co-edited the *Random House Anthology of New York Poets* and the *Whole Word Catalogue #2.*

All that said, or enumerated—and there really are others,

too—to me, one of Ron's most attractive qualities as a writer and person is his modesty. Or maybe the word is humility. Or grace. I don't have to tell you how rare all those are these days. I don't mean that in his heart of hearts he isn't aware of his own worth, or that the modesty is false, or that, like the rest of us, he doesn't have his competitive side. I mean that he is always generous, never superior; he takes things in stride, the good and the bad; the prizes are welcome but they're accompanied by some embarrassment too, especially if too much is made of them. I'm not sure the following is the most telling example, but I'll end with a tiny anecdote relating to the translating. I've always loved his version of Apollinaire's famous poem "Zone," and years ago told him I got a kick out of his solution to what seemed to me an impossible challenge. About halfway through, the poem begins a series of jumps from one remembered place and experience to another; a specific Dutch memory produces the following rhymed couplet (bear with me):

> Te voici à Amsterdam avec une jeune fille que tu trouves
> belle et qui est laide
> Elle doit se marier avec un étudiant de Leyde

Ron told me he had found it close to impossible to translate these lines, finally coming up with something he hoped worked but remained unsure about. The "te" or "you" is Apollinaire talking to himself, and you'll note the change of venue: from Leiden to The Hague:

> Here you are in Amsterdam with a girl that you find

> beautiful and who is a hag
> She's supposed to marry a student in Den Haag

To me that's poetry *gained* in translation. *Hag* is a wonderful word in a poem (both Apollinaire-esque and a lot better than "ugly"— and try to find a Dutch city that rhymes with that!), and the rhyme with *Den Haag* is audacious and delightful. But I was struck by Ron's lingering uncertainty, one of our very best translators *still* worrying over whether he had really brought it off. To me, that's one aspect of his humility and one reason he and his work are so engaging. I like to imagine that Robert Frost, complicated as *he* was, would have eventually gotten it, and been delighted, as we are, to have his medal in Ron's possession.

[Presented at PSA Award Ceremony, April 10, 2018]

News, Poetry and Poplars
for Ann Lauterbach

It may sound like a cop-out, but I'm of several minds about this topic,* like a tree in which there are several blackbirds. I used to feel that the extravagant claims made for poetry by Stevens and Williams, to name only two, had an ironic undercurrent of desperation. So few take poetry seriously, ever, that they went to extremes to ensure its survival, never mind its importance in the general scheme. Of course, Auden's "For poetry makes nothing happen" contributed to my feeling, with its quasi-logical "For" seeming to brook no debate.

As part of an introduction to a reading by John Ashbery at The Poetry Project in 2009, I made a small pitch for an Ashbery Nobel. I wasn't, of course, alone in thinking it was high time, or that the fly in the ointment was Ashbery's presumed lack of engagement with the big issues. What I said was, "To me, and I believe many others, there's no writer whose poems are more engaged with what it means to be human. Poetry sadly, hopefulness notwithstanding, doesn't make much happen. But it does show us to ourselves, which I would suggest is more vital these days than it has ever been, and has a far more vital relation to the material that poetry is often supposed to be engaged with, than ever before." This, of course, preceded the careening handbasket that the country, and increasingly the world, is finding itself unable to change the course of or jump off.

Part of me continues to think Auden was right. Another part thinks that Williams's hyperbole isn't as hyperbolic as it used to seem; that what so many miss by not attending to poetry is precisely the humanity that is so strikingly missing now in relations between people (real as well as virtual), nations, chains of reasoning, causes and effects, etc. A third part of me, part two notwithstanding, has a hard time believing poetry can help with any of it.

I do like to think that poetry has an existence beyond "the valley of its making" (where Stevens the insurance executive did tamper, but almost no one else), but in a society where it is increasingly difficult to find literature courses in English Departments (!), it is difficult to imagine poetry providing the news or solace Williams or Stevens or Pound envisioned, or the range of pleasures it, like all the arts, embodies. Maybe the fundamental concern, like a grove of Binsey poplars which the developer's axe has *unselved*, is that politics or government is viewed as an end in itself rather than a way to help people live the best lives they can, on which topic there is reason to believe poems have some relevance, as difficult as that can be to get at.

[*Brooklyn Rail*, "Why Poets Now?" Critics Page,
ed. Ann Lauterbach, April 4, 2018]

On Tony Towle's Frank O'Hara
Award-Winning Book *North*

ss   The muse at daybreak stuttering, informs my bed

cf   as Wyoming would slide down the coast of Norway

3b   The bacon too carries on its modest love affair

rf   The Allegorical Figure of Brooklyn is right here

1b   What amusing solids. Several explain the world

c   Satan: Since you deal only with your own activity

lf   after a reading waiting for Aphrodite

2b   Coleridge has told you how poignantly he felt

p   I am the salt air and the dazzling sunshine

****

dh   As far as going to bed with everyone goes

[2019]

50-ish Words on Jim Tate's "Storm"

The breath of fresh air that accompanies all of Jim Tate's poems is fittingly colder in "Storm," the outrageous gusts of language and subject quietly outrageous—and utterly convincing, like the snow that

    visits us,
    taking little bits of us with it

(for James Tate Website, 2021)

For Gary Lenhart Memorial

Gary and Louise were friends and fellow Upper West Siders before Katie was born, and before the family moved to Vermont and Dartmouth. I think Katie inherited our daughter's toy stove. Although I can't remember when or whose idea it was, after the move north, Gary and I began a snail-mail correspondence which continued till he died, I would say for at least 15 or 20 years.

Gary was a wonderful, elegant letter writer—prose writer in general—as well as a fine poet, and I always felt challenged to live up to his standard. I can't imagine our letters would interest outsiders the way, say, Jimmy Schuyler's do; but we got a great kick out of them, receiving as well as replying with gossip about poets, book recommendations (interestingly not nearly as much to do with poetry as fiction and nonfiction), reactions to current national and world situations, rueful often funny comments about the woebegone Red Sox or Mets, half-joking half-serious reports on the silly policies our respective schools had unaccountably put in place, reports on what our beloved kids were doing, reports on the doings of the poetry schmoes, et al. Some years ago, I included a big bunch of

Gary's letters in my Beinecke archive; there are a lot more by now.

Gary and I were friends at a distance; I didn't know him nearly as well as, say, Greg Masters did. But I found him—this is a cliché but I really mean it—a special person: modest, unassuming, reserved if not shy, but smart, perceptive and knowledgeable, with a great sense of humor and a love for his wife, daughter and friends palpable to all who knew him. In the mid '70s, or possibly a bit later, when we were both still going to almost every Wednesday night Project reading, we used to get a ride home fairly often from the writer/translator Murat Nemet-Najat, who was a good friend of Gary's and whom I knew too, especially through the summer poets parties at his house in Bronxville. Since he lived far from the Church, Murat drove in for readings, and he got in the habit of dropping us off on his way home. It's hard for me to remember when I've had so much fun on a regular basis. Gary and Murat too, I think. Of course we trashed (in a nice way of course!) as much as praised what we had just seen, but mostly it was letting off all sorts of poetic and other steam and laughing our heads off, with quiet, reserved Gary laughing as uproariously as we did. I think I looked forward to our rides as much as the readings.

As most of you know, Gary edited and co-edited a couple of very good poetry magazines. The one he did on his own, *Transfer*, meant a lot to me. Among other things, in one issue he published the second set of my baseball lineup poems, which were hardly known at the time; the first set had been self-published via mimeograph and staples and given away some years before and I don't know if anyone apart from a small group of poets around the Project was aware of them. Later on, partly but not only to thank him, I wrote a lineup poem which I dedicated to him; it was a second- or even third-order lineup, possibly the most complex I ever did, and partly, though no one could possibly have known, a testimony to Gary's intelligence, baseball and otherwise. Instead of pets or raw vegetables or philosophers in a batting order and playing specific positions, the one to him consisted of "Errata" relating to previously published lineups. Change *this* to *this*—batting sixth and playing right field.

I miss everything about Gary, his intelligence, his wit, his enthusiasm, his letters, his company. I'll finish by reading one of my favorites among his poems, "So Big," from *Father and Son Night*, published in 1999 by Hanging Loose.

[Presented at The Poetry Project, May 1, 2022]

Interview with Yasmine Shamma [Excerpt]*

Yasmine: I wonder if you might linger for a moment on what it felt like to be trying to establish your voice in what to me sounds like a cacophony of voices, you know, a big party on the Lower East Side. But you weren't on the Lower East Side were you?

Charles: Sorry to sound like a broken record, but "establishing my voice" sounds like critical talk, not the way I would have looked at things then—or how I would describe my situation now. I met the other poets who were roughly my age, published regularly in Project magazines, gave a reading there every two years; also taught a workshop and was on the Project Advisory Board. I did feel like something of an outsider—along, I think, with Tony [Towle] and Paul [Violi], and a few others too, e.g., Alan Kaplan, David Shapiro—partly because I arrived at the Project a little later than those I saw as the central group (Berrigan, Waldman, Warsh, Padgett, Fagin, Mayer, etc.) and partly because I was on the Upper West Side 40 minutes away by subway. But I don't recall thinking much about establishing my voice. As to the big party and being a part of it, I wasn't into drugs the way a lot of the poets were, I didn't take part in the regular poker games at George Schneeman's on St. Mark's Place, and I wasn't close enough to collaborate on a poem or poem/painting at a moment's notice. The Wednesday readings always started late and, with a big break between readers, ended late, and I usually just felt like going home!

Yasmine: I have not heard of the poker games! I've heard of lots of things, but not poker games.

Charles: Oh yeah, there were regular poker games. Yes, mostly, I think, at George and Katie Schneeman's apartment, in the same building as Anne [Waldman] and Lewis [Warsh] were in. George also did paintings of a number of the poets, with and without clothes on.

Yasmine: Are you friendly with Bob Rosenthal?

Charles: I never really knew him. Actually I knew Godfrey only a bit up until, say, the past 15 years.

Yasmine: And were you familiar or friendly with John Koethe? Because that's the other person who has come to mind while you're talking.

Charles: He's a friend now, though I hardly knew him before he moved to Milwaukee to teach philosophy. We get together for a drink when he comes into the city—which prior to Covid was fairly regularly. In addition to a poetry connection, we have a sort of philosophy connection. I have several philosophers in my family (daughter, son-in-law, cousins, high school classmate) and John knows them all. John's written generously about me and I once contributed a little something to a philosophy paper he wrote. We don't write at all alike—his early NYS leanings are by now far in the past—but we're great admirers of one another's work. He certainly has peripheral connections to the New York poets, most clearly to Ashbery, and [you were speaking of education] among those of my generation he takes the prize: Princeton, Harvard PhD, Distinguished Prof. of Philosophy (retired) at the U. of Wisconsin, Milwaukee. Pretty sure he doesn't feel he belongs as a poet (though he owes a lot to Ashbery), but he knows a lot about the poets we've been talking about. For a long time his poetry has been on the linear side—really mainstream, even though he's far more interesting than most in that category. Godfrey, Koethe and Doug Crase (who also comes out of Ashbery) were at Princeton together.

Yasmine: When I was writing my monograph, someone said at one point you have to define what you're talking about, you know? What do you mean when you say New York School? And, of course, the whole book is saying well if there is this kind of form there, then I think it should count as New York School. But I also had to offer an introductory definition. And at the time, I resorted to something really flippant that I think I wrote in five minutes and I didn't go back to on purpose which was that if you happened to be in New York City writing poetry during these two decades, the '60s and '70s depending on which school, and you happened to know or like the way Frank O'Hara wrote, and maybe knew someone who actually knew him, then you were New York School. Or, you know, read a poem at The Poetry Project, eventually. And I don't know how much I hold to that definition anymore, but with people like John Koethe actually that definition holds for them insofar as they had that direct contact with the first generation, but the poetry itself no longer has anything to do with, for lack of a more specific word, that vibe.

Charles: My reaction—instant reaction—would be that *defining*—or being unable to define, which is more to the point—is precisely what your book is about! I.e., a definition really isn't possible, but here are a number of ways the poets themselves view the situation. A lot more meaningful, I would argue, than the heading of "Street Poetry," which has application to some of the poets like Berrigan and Myles and Godfrey (with important nuances and qualifications) but by no means all or even most.

Yasmine: No, I don't even agree with my definition anymore. The academic version is that Ashbery wasn't there in the moment, you know, he went to Paris. He went to Europe. He's kind of like the Eliot of the modern American poets.

Charles: Well, I can tell you that his being abroad didn't minimize his influence on the second generation poets around the Project whatsoever! When I arrived, a bunch of poets my age were writing like John or being inspired by him in some way; he was very much in the moment. I remember poems by Brownstein, Warsh, others—even a sort of parody by Padgett that was in his first book, I think—that were testimony to Ashbery's influence. Maybe this is an exaggeration, but his being in Paris conferred some "mythic" status on him and his work as well. To me, John was the most original poet writing in English in that moment, and *Some Trees, The Tennis Court Oath,* and *Rivers and Mountains* were endlessly inspiring. Not sure if I should say this, but to me it always matters which Ashbery we're talking about. My friend Larry Fagin, who's no longer alive, was a big JA fan and published some important things of his before they were published by major publishers (as well as marvelous things like *100 Multiple Choice Questions,* which I don't know if anyone else has published?). Larry put great stock into taste, and was fond of making pronouncements, and I recall his saying at some point that Ashbery's important stuff ended in the early 1970s. I argued that "Self-Portrait in a Convex Mirror" and its book belonged, too, but Larry wouldn't agree. But I do think John's exciting, original poetry ended somewhere around then—not so surprising given that few poets do anything like their best work after 50, if not earlier. Not that he didn't write some fine poems afterwards.

Yasmine: I'm thinking too of the shorter, more recent poems, that have this kind of universal merit. Less specific, atmospheric, discursive. They just drift, in a way, not just out of the specificity of an individual urban experience but also out of the kind of materiality of the street. Which your work still does engage with, you know? So I do understand why poets who were quite influenced by Ashbery in their earlier years drifted out of what we might call the New York School and away from it because I think even Ashbery did. So that's my riff on Ashbery.

Charles: I don't think I agree about drifting away from the New York School—that sounds like a critical conceit rather than a genuinely meaningful way to view things—but I confess it's an intriguing notion.

Yasmine: So two questions: what is the New York School and what is a better title for this book?

Charles: Well, a while back I wrote a little piece that has relevance to both questions (it was supposed to be part of the Rizzoli first and second generation NYS collaborations book but turned out to be too long, or something). Here's one sentence from it that begs the question, which I argue is the best you can do. "One might say of New York School poetry, rephrasing an idea that was in the air when the first generation was coming of age, that rather than its existence preceding its essence, it supersedes it." I.e., no essence!

Yasmine: I'm just thinking of a definition of organic poetic form from Coleridge. There's a difference between form as proceeding and shape as super-induced. What you've just offered is a sense of all of these attributes that can actually be super-induced and the implication that there is nothing necessarily inherently proceeding.

Charles: Well, as I also suggested in the essay, my feeling is that the Wittgenstein notion of family resemblances may be the best, really the most accurate characterization. It goes at least some way towards clarifying an impossible situation. Poet A and poet B share this; poets C, D, and E share this; but Poet A and Poet E are very different in this respect, etc. How about *New York School Poets: A*

Family of Resemblances. One of the abiding problems is "New York." Although the first generation were all associated with NYC, really only O'Hara focused on it in his poems. Kenneth isn't a "New York" poet. Neither is Jimmy, at least mostly, or John, or Kenward, or Barbara, or Harry. Edwin partly. In my generation there's more focus on the city (maybe the O'Hara influence) but certainly not in Coolidge, Notley, Mayer, Shapiro. "School" with its inevitable connections to critics and professors is even more of a problem, the biggest one, I think. No one involved thinks they belong to a School! I can't imagine any of them/us proclaiming it, as in your working title. O'Hara's anti-academic "Personism" ("you just go on your nerve") is only one case in point, but it's a striking and important one. Of course, the *school* label in general has been problematic forever—applied to groups of artists or writers far more often in derogatory—or initially irrelevant—ways than genuinely meaningful ones. Pasted onto some poets who gravitated to NYC in the 1950s (at least many did), it seems more irrelevant than wild beasts to the Fauves! Yes, Kenneth was an academic for decades; but his teaching was as unacademic as teaching can be: that's a good part of why he was so good at it. But to get back to the issue, family resemblances à la Wittgenstein really does approach the reality of the situation. At least it seems that way to me. It's occurred to me more than once that a useful measure of inclusion in a group is who a poet's heroes are. But that doesn't seem to work if you like Schuyler and haven't much use for Koch, etc.

Yasmine: Ashbery, in his intro to the Frank O'Hara *Collected Poems* says the term "New York School" isn't helpful except that it uses the words "New York" which in itself contains this sense of, he uses the word "kaleidoscope". I think he says that kaleidoscope of variegated experiences, you know, something to imply the variousness of being a New York City human being. Another poet, I'm forgetting who, called it the public/private experience of walking down the street in New York City—that you are always operating on, or traveling between, these two poles. There is no soul there. There can't be. You're too busy traveling.

Charles: So you're responding to the word essence when you say soul?

Yasmine: Yeah, sorry, I swapped them out. I have to say, when I started talking to you, I was like "that voice sounds so familiar", and I don't know from where and I realized halfway through that you sound a lot like Kenneth Koch. I've just listened to so many of his poems read out loud. So I just wanted to share that with you.

Charles: I thought he was a wonderful reader of poetry. But I never thought I sounded like him! I'm going to have to tell his wife, Karen.

Yasmine: I'm sure she'll like that. But if you listen to any of those earlier recordings, it's very familiar.

[*For *The Oral History of the New York School of Poetry*, forthcoming]

Acknowledgments

A number of these poems and prose pieces appeared in the following publications and are reprinted by permission of the publishers. The author is grateful to all concerned, and regrets any omissions.

I

Interview with Martin Stannard was published in the online magazine *Litter* (UK, July 2021)

II

En Face, in collaboration with artist Trevor Winkfield, was published by MAB Books in 2021.

Translation, in collaboration with artist Paula North, was published by The Song Cave in 2014. The originals first appeared as follows: "Poem for Trevor Winkfield," "A Note on Labor Day," and "Nocturne" in *The Year of the Olive Oil* (Hanging Loose, 1989); "French Notebook Threatened by Writing" and "Urban Landscape" in *New and Selected Poems* (Sun & Moon, 1999). "Jig" was issued as a broadside by Viking Dog Press in 2006.

Other poems were published in *The Brooklyn Rail*, *Court Green*, *Hanging Loose*, *Litter* (UK), and *Poetry* (Chicago).

All translations in "First (French) Licks" are by the author.

III

"On 'Piece of a Rhapsody'": Poetry Society of America, *In Their Own Words* (online)

"90 Lines for John Ashbery's 90th Birthday": Literary Hub (online)

"Remembering John Ashbery": Library of America (online)

"News, Poetry and Poplars": *The Brooklyn Rail*

"50-ish Words on Jim Tate's 'Storm'": James Tate website

"Interview with Yasmine Shamma": forthcoming in *The Oral History of the New York School of Poetry*, eds. Rona Cran and Yasmine Shamma.

Special thanks to Trevor Winkfield for inspiration and encouragement.

About the Author

An active classical clarinetist in his youth, Charles North has lived most of his life in NYC. He began writing poems in his mid-20s. He has received two National Endowment for the Arts Creative Writing Fellowships, a Foundation for Contemporary Arts Grant, four Fund for Poetry awards, and a Poets Foundation Award. Among his twelve poetry collections, *What It Is Like: New and Selected Poems* headed NPR's Best Poetry Books of the Year (2011), and his recent collection *Everything and Other Poems* was named a *N.Y. Times* New and Noteworthy Book. Other published work includes three books of critical prose, collaborations with artists and other poets, poetry chapbooks, and the poet-painter anthologies *Broadway* and *Broadway 2*, which he edited with James Schuyler. He is Poet-in-Residence at Pace University.

Black Square Editions was started in 1999 with the intention of publishing translations of little-known books by well-known poets and fiction writers, as well as the work of emerging and established authors. After twenty-three years, we are still proceeding book by book.

Black Square Editions—a subsidiary of Off the Park Press, Inc, a tax-exempt (501c3) nonprofit organization—would like to thank the following for their support.

Tim Barry
Robert Bunker
Catherine Kehoe
Taylor Moore
Goldman Sachs
Pittsburgh Foundation Grant
Miles McEnery Gallery (New York, New York)
I.M. of Emily Mason & Wolf Kahn
Galerie Lelong & Co. (Paris, France)
Bernard Jacobson Gallery (London, England)
Saturnalia Books
& Anonymous Donors

Black Square Editions

Richard Anders *The Footprints of One Who Has Not Stepped Forth* (trans. Andrew Joron)

Andrea Applebee *Aletheia*

Eve Aschheim and Chris Daubert *Episodes with Wayne Thiebaud: Interviews*

Eve Aschheim *Eve Aschheim: Recent Work*

Anselm Berrigan *Pregrets*

Garrett Caples *The Garrett Caples Reader*

Billie Chernicoff *Minor Secrets*

Marcel Cohen *Walls (Anamneses)* (trans. Brian Evenson and Joanna Howard)

Lynn Crawford *Fortification Resort*

Lynn Crawford *Simply Separate People, Two*

Thomas Devaney *You Are the Battery*

Ming Di (Editor) *New Poetry from China: 1917–2017* (trans. various)

Joseph Donahue *Infinite Criteria*

Joseph Donahue *Red Flash on a Black Field*

Rachel Blau DuPlessis *Late Work*

Marcella Durand *To husband is to tender*

Rosalyn Drexler *To Smithereens*

Brian Evenson *Dark Property*

Jared Daniel Fagen *The Animal of Existence*

Serge Fauchereau *Complete Fiction* (trans. John Ashbery and Ron Padgett)

Jean Frémon *Painting* (trans. Brian Evenson)

Jean Frémon *The Paradoxes of Robert Ryman* (trans. Brian Evenson)

Vicente Gerbasi *The Portable Gerbasi* (trans. Guillermo Parra)

Jeanne Heuving *Indigo Angel*

Ludwig Hohl *Ascent* (trans. Donna Stonecipher)

Isabelle Baladine Howald *phantomb* (trans. Eléna Rivera)

Philippe Jaccottet *Ponge, Pastures, Prairies* (trans. John Taylor)

Ann Jäderlund *Which once had been meadow* (trans. Johannes Göransson)

Franck André Jamme *Extracts from the Life of a Beetle* (trans. Michael Tweed)

Franck André Jamme *Another Silent Attack* (trans. Michael Tweed)

Franck André Jamme *The Recitation of Forgetting* (trans. John Ashbery)

Andrew Joron *Fathom*

Andrew Joron *OO*

Robert Kelly *Linden Word*
Karl Larsson *FORM/FORCE* (trans. Jennifer Hayashida)
Hervé Le Tellier *Atlas Inutilis* (trans. Cole Swensen)
Eugene Lim *The Strangers*
Michael Leong *Cutting Time with a Knife*
Michael Leong *Words on Edge*
Gary Lutz *I Looked Alive*
Franca Mancinelli *All the Eyes that I Have Opened* (trans. John Taylor)
Michèle Métail *Earth's Horizons: Panorama* (trans. Marcella Durand)
Michèle Métail *Identikits* (trans. Philip Terry)
Albert Mobilio *Me with Animal Towering*
Albert Mobilio *Touch Wood*
Albert Mobilio *Games & Stunts*
Albert Mobilio *Same Faces*
Pascalle Monnier *Bayart* (trans. Cole Swensen)
Christopher Nealon *The Joyous Age*
María Negroni *Berlin Interlude* (trans. Michelle Gil-Montero)
Charles North *News, Poetry and Poplars*
Doug Nufer *Never Again*
John Olson *Echo Regime*
John Olson *Free Stream Velocity*
Eva Kristina Olsson *The Angelgreen Sacrament* (trans. Johannes Göransson)
Juan Sánchez Peláez *Air on the Air: Selected Poems* (trans. Guillermo Parra)
Véronique Pittolo *Hero* (trans. Laura Mullen)
Pierre Reverdy *Prose Poems* (trans. Ron Padgett)
Pierre Reverdy *Haunted House* (trans. John Ashbery)
Pierre Reverdy *The Song of the Dead* (trans. Dan Bellm)
Pierre Reverdy *Georges Braque: A Methodical Adventure* (trans. Andrew Joron
   and Rose Vekony)
Valérie-Catherine Richez *THIS NOWHERE WHERE*
Barry Schwabsky *Book Left Open in the Rain*
Barry Schwabsky *Feelings of And*
Barry Schwabsky *Heretics of Language*
Barry Schwabsky *Trembling Hand Equilibrium*
Jeremy Sigler *Crackpot*
Jørn H. Sværen *Queen of England* (trans. Jørn H. Sværen)
Genya Turovskaya *The Breathing Body of This Thought*
Matvei Yankelevich *Some Worlds for Dr. Vogt*